Amory Carter

Sawyers in America

A history of the immigrant Sawyers, who settled in New England

Amory Carter

Sawyers in America
A history of the immigrant Sawyers, who settled in New England

ISBN/EAN: 9783337152864

Printed in Europe, USA, Canada, Australia, Japan

Cover: Foto ©Andreas Hilbeck / pixelio.de

More available books at **www.hansebooks.com**

SAWYERS IN AMERICA;

— OR —

A HISTORY

OF THE

IMMIGRANT SAWYERS.

INCOMPLETE.

COMPRISING ALL OF THE WORK THAT COULD BE FOUND
AFTER THE DEATH OF THE AUTHOR.

By AMORY CARTER.

WORCESTER:
PRESS OF EDWARD R. FISKE.
1883.

SAWYERS IN AMERICA;

— OR —

A HISTORY OF THE IMMIGRANT SAWYERS,

WHO SETTLED IN NEW ENGLAND; SHOWING THEIR CONNEC-
TION WITH COLONIAL HISTORY — THE MANY THRILLING
SCENES THEY PASSED THROUGH — NARROW ESCAPES
FROM DEATH BY THE INDIANS, Etc   ALSO,
WONDERFUL INCREASE OF THE DESCEND-
ANTS OF THOMAS SAWYER, ONE OF
THE NINE FIRST SETTLERS WHO
ORGANIZED THE TOWN OF
LANCASTER AND GAVE
IT ITS NAME.

By AMORY CARTE..

OF WORCESTER, MASS.,

(WHO, BY A SAD ACCIDENT, HAS BECOME BLIND).

WORCESTER:
PRESS OF EDWARD. R. FISKE.
1883

DEDICATION.

The following work is dedicated to Hon. LORENZO SAWYER, Judge of the Northwest District U. S. Circuit Court, residing at San Francisco, California, who is a descendant of THOMAS SAWYER, senior, of Lancaster, Mass., and of the seventh generation of the Sawyer Genealogy. To him will the Sawyers be greatly indebted for important information which the editor could not otherwise obtain this side of the Rocky Mountains, or even this side of the Mississippi Valley. His liberality has enabled the editor to bring out what otherwise could not have been done. To him is due not only the editor's thanks, but also the thanks of the whole Sawyer race, through all coming times. He has helped preserve a record which would have, but for his assistance, been lost forever. His likeness will be presented in its proper place in his branch of the Sawyer family, with a narrative of his life history. Also, thanks are due to Hon Philetus Sawyer, U. S. Senator from Wisconsin, who is also a descendant from Thomas Sawyer, of Lancaster. To him the Sawyer race are also indebted for a liberal contribution to assist in bringing out this historical work.

The Editor is also indebted to Jonathan Sawyer, Esq., of Dover, for valuable contribution to aid in bringing out the work.

PREFACE.

To compose a history of the Immigrant SAWYERS seems like entering a dark cave and searching for treasure under the accumulated rubbish of time. Two centuries have finished their scrolls — been rolled up and laid by — while the finger on the dial-plate of the third century is fast approaching the zenith; and still the history of the Immigrant Sawyers is unwritten. It can now be done only by picking up fragments by the wayside, coupling them with tradition and carrying them out by the memory. It is no desirable task, and yet it seems necessary in order to preserve a meritorious history. It is entered upon with confidence, and unhesitatingly, trusting in the charity and forbearance of the people toward a blind man. I write what I have accumulated, what I have heard, and much of what I personally know. If I interest posterity, I shall be satisfied.

HISTORY.

TO TRACE up the history of the first emigrant Sawyers, there are three sources to refer to :—Incidental records, traditional history, and the memory. The most authentic record seems to be " Savage's Genealogy of Old Settlers." He finds Edmund Sawyer at Ipswich in 1636, and removed to York before 1661. He next finds Thomas and Edward at Rowley, and William at Salem in 1643. Thomas went to Lancaster the same year. William went from Salem to Wenham, thence to Newbury, and settled there in 1645. He had twelve children ;— John, Samuel, Ruth, Sarah, William, Mary, Stephen, Francis, and four others who died while young.

Edward was at Rowley in 1643, married Mary, and had a son John, and probably Ezekiel who was a soldier in the company called the " Flower of Essex," and killed by the Indians at Bloody Brook, Sept. 18, 1675.

The descendants of William and Edward were probably scattered through Essex, Suffolk, and Norfolk Counties, and perhaps some in Middlesex. But all west of Middlesex appear to have descended from Thomas Sawyer of Lancaster. One tradition says that three emigrant brothers came over together ; that they came from Lincolnshire, England, and sailed as passengers in a ship commanded by Capt. Parker ;—that their names were

2

Edmund, William and Thomas, and that they arrived in 1636. Here seems to be a discrepancy between Savage's Genealogy and tradition, for Savage does not find William and Thomas until 1643, and with Thomas was Edward, not Edmund, as is proved by the fact that the Rowley records show that a piece of land was set off to Thomas Sawyer, and another to Edward Sawyer in 1643, one of the boundaries of each lot being upon the Ocean. Thus showing that the three brothers were William, Edward and Thomas, and that they came over in 1643. Edmund came over. seven years earlier. Whether he was brother to the other three cannot be ascertained, but all agree that Thomas Sawyer was at Lancaster in 1643. And the chief Sawyer interest is centered in Thomas Sawyer and his descendants, who have multiplied to thousands. To fully understand the history of Thomas Sawyer and his descendants it is necessary to recall a considerable amount of colonial history.

The first decade after the landing of the pilgrims was a somewhat doubtful success. But the second decade changed the weight in the balance. The peninsular of Boston had been discovered, as also the Massachusetts Bay, and the fertile land lying round the Bay which was eagerly seized by persons desiring homes, and was soon occupied by permanent settlers. That fact was discovered by the persons who deemed themselves born to rule. They immediately applied to Parliament, or to the English Crown, for a government Charter under which they ruled, with the title of " The Government of Massachusetts Bay." Under that Charter a regular governmental *retinue* was appointed by the Massachusetts Bay Company, who held the Charter in their own right. Thus a regular aristocratical government was set in motion. But the government had many difficulties to contend with. They had to govern a colony which had established a democratic government for themselves. But to avoid the ire of the British Crown they admitted themselves to be subjects of Great Britian. The settlers had considered themselves as being subjects of the democratic government. They were principally dissenters from the established church of England. They established themselves in little democracies, representing in size the parishes into which the shire towns of England were divided. They managed their own ecclesiastical affairs, and each settlement organized into a little community which they called a town. Hence the Massachusetts Bay Government found a very difficult community to govern. The English system of Government was not adapted to this colony. So they concluded, like the old fable, that circumstances alter cases. The English system of government must be thrown around the democratic system. Thus many little wheels within one great wheel. Then the wheels were set in motion,—at least the great wheel began to revolve around the little wheels which were already in motion. Soon after this, wealth began to cast its eyes abroad, and here was a place of profitable investment. And there was another set of persons who seemed to follow English colonies, as rats are said to always follow wherever the human race go. They were adventurers who came in pursuit of wealth to fill their coffers. They did not come to settle. They merely squatted for a time, and that time only while they could profitably ply their trade. One of those out-post trading houses was at Watertown, and thither went Sholan, sachem of the Nashawots, to trade his furs. While at Watertown he recommended to Thomas King the valley of the Nashaway as a good place to form a settlement,—said he owned the land, and would sell it, and would like to have the white people come and settle beside him, and be friends and neighbors to him. Soon after, Thomas King and some associates mounted their horses and started out on a tour of inspection, or observation. They had to ford the Sudbury and Assabet rivers, and rode up through what is now Stow into Bolton, and ascended Waterquattuck Hill ; from thence they looked down upon the Nashua valley. There lay spread out before them a beautiful intervale clothed with nature's green carpet inter. spersed with flowers, with a silvery line of bright waters winding through the midst,—the same now called Still River,—interspersed here and there with tall elms and hickory trees, they being the most hardy kinds of trees, and able to withstand the overflowing of the waters of the river during the spring and fall freshets. The table-lands above were covered with trees waving their green foliage in the breeze, and the lands being free of rocks and easy of cultivation, it seemed to them like a new Garden of Eden.

They then rode down and, crossing the intervale, fording the South branch of the Nashua River, rode up on George Hill, then looking back and taking a retrospective view, it seemed truly a Garden of Eden without its flowers and minus Adam and Eve. From there they rode up into what is now Sterling, to the residence of Sholan, whose wigwam was near Waushacum Pond. They made a trade with him for a strip of land ten miles long and eight miles broad lying on either side of the river, and history or tradition, perhaps both, say took a Deed of the same, and it was specified in the Deed that the Indians should not be disturbed in their hunting, fishing and planting. It is also stated that the government of Massachusetts Bay sanctioned the purchase.

The first occupancy seems to have been by three persons who had gifts of land as an inducement to commence a settlement. The names of those three persons were Richard Linton, Lawrence Waters, and Thomas Ball. Thomas Sawyer is said to have been there in 1643. Whether he remained is not so sure, but he was there in 1647, and took the oath and covenant required of a citizen by the Government of Massachusetts Bay, in company with John Prescott, James Atherton, and one other.

Thomas Sawyer married Mary, the daughter of John Prescott, and their son, Thomas Sawyer, Jr., was born in July, 1649, and was probably the first white child born in Lancaster. In 1653 nine persons assembled, being settlers, and organized the town, giving it the name of Lancaster.

The settlement went on increasing, and they lived at peace with the Indians for about twenty years, the Indians actually being useful in preparing and establishing their homes. They had raised up families of children, many of whom had arrived nearly to manhood. They knew no other home ; they had always lived in peace and quiet with the Indians, but there now came a sad change. The Indians became unfriendly. There appeared a war-cloud in the distance. Sad forebodings came as if upon the breeze. The realities were these : Massasoit had died, and his mantle rightfully fell upon Wamsutta, his eldest grandson. The government had made a treaty with Massasoit which was faithfully maintained for fifty years. The government, before the death of Massasoit, sought to obligate Wamsutta and Mettecomet, his grandsons, to become citizens of that government, and had wrought upon their pride by giving them great names. Wamsutta was given the name of the great Macedonian Emperor, Alexander, and Mettacomet was called Phillip, or King Phillip, whether of Macedon or Spain does not so readily appear. Those names were intended to work upon their vanity, thus inducing them to become citizens, they not knowing what a trap they were being caught in. After the death of Massasoit, Alexander was required to submit to the government as a citizen. He knew that he was rightful ruler over the land which his grandfather ruled. He did not obey the government, but went on a visit to the Narragansett Indians. He afterwards returned to his own house. The government sent a posse to bring him before the magistrates. When the posse arrived they found Wamsutta dining with his body-guard in his house. The body-guard had stacked their arms in the yard. The posse slipped in between them and their arms, thus making them prisoners. The leader then invited Wamsutta to go aside with him and hold a conference, which he did, and when well aside, the leader presented a pistol to his breast and ordered him to go with him to the magistrates or die on the spot. Wamsutta's interpreter being present, he advised him to go, and he went. The magistrates put him under such obligations as they chose. Wamsutta, alias Alexander, being now a prisoner, his feelings were much wrought upon, and he fell sick, and they sent him home to his own house, but kept him under guard until he died. The rightful authority of Massasoit now fell upon his second son, Mettacomet. He considered that his brother's death was caused by the ill-treatment of the whites. The government now summoned Mettecomet, alias King Philip, to appear before the magistrates. He refused to obey the Governor, as he was a subject of King Charles. Said Philip: "When my brother Charles comes, I am ready for him." Very significant words. Charles was sovereign of England; Philip was rightful Sovereign of the territory ruled over by his grandfather Massasoit. He was too wily to be caught napping, and fled to the arms of his countrymen, the Wampanoags, where the whites could not catch him.

He had not intended to compromise the rights inherited from his grandfather. The Government of Massachusetts Bay had intended to usurp those rights. Thus they were at natural war. Philip saw the condition, and knew it must come, and began to prepare for it. He saw that his people had been driven into a corner. Their lands had been gotten from them, not for a mess of pottage, but for little trinkets and gew-gaws which pleased the eyes of the Indian squaws. The Government defended and maintained all such deceitful trades, and pretended purchases. Hence the Indians had not land enough left on which to raise their corn and spread their blankets. Philip saw that it was life or death with the Indians, and began to prepare for war. He could neither read nor write, but he had a secretary by the name of Sarsamon who wrote for him. His secretary turned traitor and informed the whites of his designs. For such conduct the Indians seized and executed him. The whites in retaliation seized three Indians and executed them. The young men among the Indians could be restrained no longer, even by King Philip. They commenced the war by general massacre, as was the Indian custom.

Philip was now drawn into the war a year before he intended to have been. He went to the Narragansetts, the Nipmucs, and the Nashuas, and being a man of great eloquence he persuaded them to join him in a war of extermination. He perceived that that must be the natural result, and prepared for it during winter. The Government organized mounted bodies of armed men. They ranged about during the winter, falling upon bodies of Indians wherever found. But the Indians knew the land, and fled into swamps where mounted men could not reach them. In the spring Philip began war in good earnest.

Lancaster being the most isolated and exposed out-post within his lines, the inhabitants of that town received the first shock of war. Philip entered Lancaster in person with a band of 1500 warriors. They made their attack at five different points at the same time. Many of the people who were out of doors and exposed were killed, but their houses were of the primitive style, built of hewn timbers piled one above the other, and locked together at the corners. They were naturally garrison houses, having no glass windows; the openings were small and served well for port holes for musketry. They were bullet proof, and the Indians could not approach to set them on fire without being shot down from the port holes. The Indians were kept at bay by the defendants in their houses for nearly two days.

The second day their efforts were principally concentrated on the garrison house of Mr. Rawlinson, in which there were from forty to fifty persons, some 15 or more being armed men ; the rest women and children. The Indians could not approach the house without being shot down. At length they got up a strategy ; they filled a cart with combustible materials, some say it was flax, though it might have been hay. They set it on fire in the rear,—then running it backward against the house, set the house on fire. The people were driven out by the flames, and a general massacre of the men ensued. The men were all slain, except one who escaped, and two or three whom the Indians reserved for torture. The women and children were all led away into captivity.

That garrison house stood on the South side of the North River, near New Boston, in Lancaster. Probably the garrison house of Mr. Rawlinson was used for the double purpose of a family residence and a place for religious meetings, as he was the minister of the place ; he himself was at Boston seeking military aid.

Capt. Wadsworth, who was then stationed at Marlborough, hearing of the distress at Lancaster, hastened to their relief, and stationed his soldiers in the different garrison houses, for the protection of the people. They remained there about six weeks, and could not venture out night or day, without endangering their lives. Capt. Wadsworth lost one of his soldiers while thus quartered.

The inhabitants petitioned the Government for assistance, stating that they were thus confined and their lives endangered. Marlborough being threatened, Capt. Wadsworth was obliged to return, and the inhabitants all fled away with the soldiers. All the property of the town was then destroyed, except two isolated garrison houses. Those two houses still remain, and are in good condition for occupancy.

Thomas' Sawyer, whose house was in the most central part of the Indian raid, seems to have escaped with all his numerous family, with the exception of his son Ephraim, who was killed at or near the house of his grandfather, John Prescott.

Lancaster remained desolate for some three years. Where the family of Thomas' Sawyer resided during that time is not evident. But it is certain that they re-appeared on the scene at the re-building of the town, and took a conspicuous part in the growth and prosperity of the town during the next 30 years.

After the re-building, Lancaster was the home of peace, plenty, and prosperity until 1705, or until the accession of Charles II to the throne of England, and a new war broke out between England and France. At the North of New England, bordering on the St. Lawrence River, was a people of French origin,—they were French colonists. The French colonies had always fraternized with the Indians, with the exception of one small portion, where the French sided with one tribe of Indians which was at war with another. Ever after they were at peace with the Indians, and many of the colonists took to themselves Indian wives, instead of doing as the English did at Jamestown, where they sent to England and obtained a shipload of women, who were brought over and sold to the planters, in exchange for tobacco, etc., with which the ship was re-freighted and sent back. The amalgamation of the French and Indians had raised up a set of half-breeds, who inherited the hatred of their fathers,—the French and English having always been enemies,—and also of their mothers, many of whom fled from the English colonies, having had many of their fathers and brothers killed in the King Philip War.

The French authorities stimulated the body of French half-breeds and Indians to make a raid on the British colonies. They started with 700 men for Hadley. The citizens had anticipated trouble from the Indians, and had procured from the Government a company of soldiers, which was called the "Flower of Essex," for their protection, and were building a stockade fort for their defence, intending to winter there. They had grain in Deerfield which they wished to procure, and sent teams for the purpose, and also sent the company of soldiers to protect the teams. The grain was loaded and started for home, the soldiers protecting it the while. Going through a swamp near a brook they fell into an ambuscade of Indians. The soldiers and teamsters were all killed, except one soldier and one teamster, who escaped to Hadley and carried the news. The brook where the massacre took place has always been known since as "Bloody Brook." The citizens of Hadley made preparations to receive the Indians. The next morning a man who seemed to have military knowledge, appeared, and assuming command of the citizens arranged them in such a state of defence that when the Indians came they met with such a warm reception that they soon beat a retreat. The stranger who thus appeared was never seen afterwards. He was supposed to have been Lord Goff, one of the two judges who fled from England on the accession of Charles the II. to the throne, they having before condemned Charles the I. to the scaffold, and their heads were sought to pay the forfeit. They were said to have been secreted in an upper room of a house in Hadley during the rest of their lives. They had a blind passage from their room down into a dark cellar where they could secrete themselves if search had been made for them. While they were on their way to Hadley they were secreted under a bridge while their pursuers passed over without discovering them. There were 700 French and Indians, 200 of whom returned to Canada. 500 of them changed their course to Lancaster. When they arrived there Lancaster again became the scene of a bloody massacre. The house of Peter Joslin was first entered, in which two women and two children were killed. Mr. Joslin himself returning from work, found his family weltering in their blood. Many of the citizens were shot down in their fields, and the inhabitants generally had to defend themselves in their garrison houses.

Thomas' Sawyer's garrison proved a safe defence against the Indians. There were numbers of French, among whom was one high French officer who is said to have been mortally wounded while in Lancaster, which much exasperated them. Thomas Sawyer, Jr., with his young son, Elias,³ was taken prisoner from his own house, and in company with John Biglow, they were taken to Canada. On arriving there Biglow and young Sawyer

3

were delivered into the hands of the French Governor; but Thomas Sawyer they would not deliver up for money or any other consideration. He had been brave and caused the death of several of their number. He was destined to torture. He was taken out, fastened to a stake, the fagots placed around him ready for a fire, and the Indians were assembled ready to rend the air with their hideous cries, mingled with his groans of torture.

At this moment a man appeared as a Friar, exhibiting what he claimed to be the keys of purgatory, and told them if they tortured Sawyer he would unlock purgatory and pitch them all in. Superstition prevailed, and then unbinding Sawyer they delivered him into the hands of the French Governor.

Sawyer told the French Governor that there was a good place for a saw mill on the Chamblee River.

They were very much in need of a saw-mill, as there were none in Canada. Neither had they any man competent to build one. Sawyer proposed that he and Biglow would build a mill, and the compensation should be their freedom. The terms were accepted. In a year's time they completed the mill and received their freedom. But young Sawyer was kept another year to teach others how to keep the mill in order and run it. He was then amply rewarded and returned home.

While in Canada he formed the acquaintance of a young lady, whom he promised to go back and marry after he had visited his friends. She gave him a little brown earthen plate as a memento, which is now in the possession of Elsworth Sawyer, of Phillipston, Mass., who says that Elias regretted while on his death bed that he did not go back and marry her. Instead of marrying the Canadian lady he did marry Beatrice Houghton, grand-daughter of Ralph Houghton, who, in company with, Thomas Sawyer and seven others, organized the town of Lancaster. From that marriage descended some of the most eminent persons in the Sawyer family. The Sawyers and Houghtons intermarried extensively through seven generations at least, as will be shown hereafter.

Their home was what is now South Lancaster, and near the old homestead of Thomas Sawyer the immigrant, which was situated on the east side of the town road, leading through what was known as New Boston. Thus Thomas' Sawyer's numerous family, all escaped both Indian raids except his son Ephraim, who was killed during King Philip's war.

It may be well here, for the benefit of the future, to indicate how the King Philip war ended. It was commenced as a war of extermination — the Indians intending to exterminate the whites — but instead of that, the Indians themselves were nearly exterminated. They fought bravely for three years to defend their homes and the graves of their fathers, but superior military skill and improved weapons of warfare were too formidable, and they had to succumb. Many thousands of Indians lost their lives, and the remnants of four Indian tribes fled away — part of them to the Mohawks in New York, and part of them to the west and north-west and into Canada, as has before been described. Philip himself went to the Mohawks. Supposing the war was ended, he came on a peaceful mission, with his wife and son, to visit the graves of his fathers. He was set upon by the whites, his wife and son snatched away from his side. He himself fled from his pursuers into a swamp, and being partially surrounded, like a tiger driven to bay, he sought safety by flight, and while running from the swamp was seen by an apostate Indian of his own tribe and killed by him with a shot in the back. A white man coming up, called on the Indian who had served as executioner, and ordered him to cut Philip into quarters. The Indian came up and exclaimed, "You have been a very great man and have made a great many men afraid of you, and now I will chop you to pieces." He chopped Philip's head off and cut his body into quarters. The quarters were hung up around on the trees; the head was carried down to Weymouth and stuck up on a pole and remained there for weeks to gratify the curiosity of those religious puritans. One of the hands of King Philip was sent to Boston as a trophy for that christian Governor, Winthrop, and his under-magistrates. They did not get the rightful ruler of the territory governed by Massasoit, whom they had summoned before them some three years before, but they did get his dead hand, and they got his young son, sent him to the West Indies and sold him as a slave. He lived and died there as a slave; and thus ended the dynasty of Massasoit, much unlike the dauphin heir of the French throne. The King Philip war was brought on by the usurpation of the government of Massachusetts Bay. .

The citizens of Lancaster, among whom was Thomas' Sawyer, one of the nine first settlers, were among those first to suffer — the innocent for the guilty, as usually is the case. They were tillers of the land — they were building up homes — they had lived in peace and friendship with their Indian neighbors, and had raised up large families of children, and those children knew no other home. They had been brought into the scenes of horror which we have described by the acts of the government. Thomas' Sawyer, whose history mainly we are now attempting to give, seemed to have been one of the most conspicuous of the early citizens of Lancaster. His garrison was always invulnerable, and hence his family all escaped massacre except one, who was not at home. His garrison stood within view of the most thrilling scenes, namely, the capture of Mr. Rollinson's garrison. There was one tall witness which, could it have spoken, might have given a record of scenes that mortal pen could never have described. It was a monster elm that stood some distance east of the Rollinson massacre. If it was not king of the forest, it was monarch of all it surveyed, and that was no small amount of territory. Its subjects were no mean specimens of the inhabitants of the forest. They were scattered over a splendid intervale and standing in all their pristine grandeur; they were composed of elm and hickory, and that great elm overtowered them all. I knew it well while it was in its highest glory. Probably there had been many an Indian council-fire held under that tree for more than one century before the white man's foot trod on the soil of Lancaster. Its spreading branches must have covered nearly one hundred feet in diameter. In passing by it one day I beheld a sorrowful sight: more than a third of that tree lay prostrate on the ground, the eastern branch had broken off some twenty feet from the ground, and it was being cut up preparatory to removal. There were blocks that had been cut up by the cross-cut saw which were apparently two feet in diameter, where, if the tree were standing, it would have been forty or fifty feet above the ground. The next time I passed by, it had been all cleared away, and the two remaining branches appeared to stand as mourners for their friend who had gone; but they did not have to mourn long, for when I again passed by, they, too, were gone, and the splintered trunk stood pointing into the air, indicating the place where the branches had been. When next I passed, the trunk had disappeared, and there was nothing left but the stump which bore the mark of the wood-cutter's axe. That stump must have been nine or ten feet in diameter. I thought it to have been the king of forest trees, but I had not then heard of California.

It seems to be well to have it understood that the Indians did cultivate the soil, and were not entirely nomadic, as is now commonly believed. Drake's history records the fact that Gov. Bradford sailed around Cape Cod in a vessel and purchased two hogsheads of corn of the Indians; also, that King Philip had one thousand acres growing at Mount Hope when he fled to the Wampanaugs, who were his countrymen, to escape arrest by Gov. Winthrop, and the whites confiscated his corn to their own use. Thus he sacrificed his summer residence at Fowling Pond and his winter residence at Mount Hope, on Cape Cod. The war that he commenced was in defence of an inalienable right descended to him from his father, Massasoit. Whether it be called faith or Providence, the right was on his side. Who shall say that Providence did a great wrong? Let the Puritans answer.

It is said that the deed given by Sholan to Thomas King and associates, conveying the territory of Lancaster, contained the stipulation that the Indians should not be molested in their hunting, fishing and planting, thus showing that they were cultivators of the soil, and showing that Sholan had a permanent residence near Waushacum pond. The first settlers of Lancaster kept the faith with the Indians and lived in peace with them for twenty years. It is evident that they had nothing to do in bringing on the war with King Philip. The cause of the war rested with the government, and Lancaster being an outpost, received the first shock of war. Among the innocent who thus suffered, Thomas Sawyer was one of the most prominent, and by his superior ability, sagacity and skill he saved his family and himself from destruction and death, and thereby became one of the most important bases in the foundation of New England wealth and prosperity. Of him and his descendants it is the purpose here mainly to speak.

They were an unprecedentedly prolific race. They probably outnumber any other family race throughout New England, unless it be the Wilders; and no one family of them could equal that of Thomas' Sawyer. They were a race of universal mechanics. They were not born, as Donnelly of Wisconsin declared in the House of Representatives, " that the Washburns were born with ' M. C.' stamped on their backs." If the Sawyers were not born with saws in their hands, the saws came very readily to their hands, and they were skilful in their use; in fact, they were real Sawyers. Every town, village, road, and lane throughout New England bears witness of their skill and industry. The water-wheels and the machinery by which they are moved daily repeat their requiem. The saw-mill on the Chamblee river in Canada repeats the requiem of Thomas' Sawyer, who purchased his liberty as a captive of war by building the same, and many of the other mills in Lancaster join in the refrain, giving honor to the master-builder who superintended the building of their foundations, and whose remains now lie mingling with the soil from which they received their nourishment and growth, in return for which, industry and skill has contributed so much to her material wealth and happiness.

As a race, they were natural mechanics. I have known them as millwrights, wheelwrights, blacksmiths, coppersmiths, carpenters, coopers, and, in fact, interested in all the mechanical skill required in New England life. They had a natural proclivity for water-power, many of them owning mills, and one in particular, in Bolton, as a water-power for building mills and machinery. His name is Joel, and he began life as a watch-maker and repairer, but he soon changed his employment to that of a mill-wright. He told me that he had built wheels from one-eighth of an inch to twelve feet in diameter. He is now over seventy years of age, and working busily at his trade. He had a brother named George, who was a building-mover; another one named Joseph, who was a store-keeper, and the youngest brother worked many years as a miller. Another Sawyer built a mill on the road leading from Bolton to Stowe, and the mill is now in the hands of his descendants. Another mill was built in New Hampshire by John Sawyer, who was probably a descendant of Edmund Sawyer who settled in York (now Maine), he having lived in Hampsted, then in Massachusetts, and is now in Maine. Those mills are now in the hands of the Sawyer family, one of whom, Wm. H. Sawyer, is now keeping a lumber-yard in Worcester, and he said to me, " I never knew a Sawyer who could not take care of himself." A communication from him will be found in these pages hereafter.

There was a set of mills in the north part of Boylston, built by Joseph Sawyer, who was probably grandson of Thomas' Sawyer, Jr., of Lancaster. The mills have been removed and the power is now used for manufacturing purposes. The village is now known as " Sawyer's Mills." The eldest son of the immigrant, Thomas' Sawyer, was known as Thomas Sawyer, Jr. ; he was the before-named returned prisoner from Canada ; his oldest son, Bezaleel,[2] died before Thomas Sawyer, Jr., made his last will. The next son, William,[3] settled in Bolton, and owned about three hundred acres of land, situated in front of the old meeting-house in Bolton. The names of William Sawyer's sons have been discovered almost by accident. They were found in the hands of Mrs. Silas Sawyer, of Berlin ; the list was made by her mother, whose maiden name was Whitcomb, of Bolton ; no connection with my mother, who was daughter of Capt. Josiah Sawyer, of Berlin. The list reads as follows, viz. : Benjamin, Dr. Israel, Joseph, William, Josiah, Uriah and Aholiab. I cannot trace the whole of their descendants, but those of William and Josiah will be found hereafter, as they are very numerous. Aholiab went to Templeton and became the parent of a large family of Sawyers. William had a son Joseph, who was the father of Joseph, George, Joel and Nathan, two of whom are now living in Bolton. One of them had a son by the name of Calvin ; he had six sons, viz. : Elijah, Silas, Oliver, Nathaniel and Daniel. Elijah, Elias and Capt. Oliver were blacksmiths ; Silas, Nathaniel and Daniel were wheelwrights. Capt. Oliver had a shop on what was called the Pan in Bolton, and was the best tool-maker of his age. I had a chopper's ax, a pair of chisels and carpenter's adze made to order by him. Elias was the inventor of a copper pump, so extensively used in New England. I used to go to his shop to procure plumbing to be done. He had a nephew, Elijah Sawyer, Jr., who was in company with him, and did most of the out-door work. His shop stood in what was known as New Boston, now known as South Lancaster. It stood nearly opposite the Thomas Sawyer, Jr., mansion house, and I am told both now exist. Daniel Sawyer I well knew, having labored with him in house-building. He had ten children. I knew three of them — the sons — whose names were Daniel, Josiah and George; two of the daughters were Hannah and Catherine. Hannah married Leonard Coburn, of Berlin. Josiah was my great-grandfather, and was parent of all the Berlin Sawyers. A communication will be found in the following pages from Joel Sawyer, before mentioned, giving further account of the Bolton Sawyers, who were from five of the sons of William Sawyer, Josiah having settled in Berlin and Aholiab in Templeton Calvin was probably the father or grandfather of Capt. Oliver Sawyer, a blacksmith and edge-tool maker of high repute in Bolton. I knew him well, having procured carpenter's tools made by him many years ago. He has a son now living in Rindge, N. H. He told me his grandfather's name was Calvin. A brother of Capt. Oliver, by the name of Elisha, who was a copper-pump manufacturer in Lancaster, I knew well, and understood he was the originator of the copper-pump business in New England.

Moses Sawyer was a grandson of Joseph Sawyer, of " Sawyer's Mills," and great-grandson of Thomas Sawyer, Jr., of Lancaster. He had a son Ephraim, as was proved by a deed given by Ephraim and Mary Sawyer conveying a right in inherited property in Sterling to the widow of Moses Sawyer, enabling her, as administratrix, to make a final conveyance of the property left by Moses Sawyer; thus showing conclusively that Moses Sawyer had a son Ephraim, the only Ephraim Sawyer known in Lancaster, except a son of Thomas Sawyer, Sen., who was killed during King Philip's war. Moses Sawyer lived in an old house in what is now Clinton. It stood on the road leading from West Boylston to Clinton. The house was recently taken down and a bundle of papers found beside the chimney in which the name of

Thomas Sawyer frequently occurred, thereby indicating his near relationship to Thomas Sawyer. There was also a commission found among the papers from The Lord High Admiralty of England, commissioning him a Lieutenant in a military company, bearing date in the year 1757. A copy of it was recently published in the *Clinton Courant.*

Moses Sawyer once owned nearly all the land on which the town of Clinton now stands, as was evidenced by twelve separate Deeds running to Moses Sawyer, which were sent in for me to examine. One of them covered a large tract, purporting to be where the Lancaster mills now stand; one deed conveyed the cottage built by Jabez Prescott, together with eighteen acres of land connected therewith. lying on the south side of the road leading from the depot, by the old Quilt factory. Another deed from John Prescott, Jr., to Moses Sawyer, covered twenty acres or more, lying on the north side of the same road, nearly opposite. That land was inherited from John Prescott, Sen., who was great-great-grandfather to Moses Sawyer, and who built the first mill ever built in Lancaster, on the spot where the Quilt factory stood, or did stand before I became blind.

The second son of Thomas Sawyer was named Ephraim, and was killed by the Indians. He had two daughters named Mary and Elizabeth. The fourth son was named Joshua, and settled in Woburn, and married Sarah Potter, and had Abigail, Joshua, Sarah, Hannah, Martha and Elizabeth; this is all I can learn of his family.

James, the fourth son, went to Pomfret, Conn., and married Mary Marble. I cannot trace him any further. Caleb, his fifth son, settled in Harvard, and Wilbur F. Sawyer, one of his descendants, now occupies the homestead. A brother of Wilbur F. Sawyer is now a Professor in Wisconsin University.

Caleb Sawyer, of Harvard, son of Thomas Sawyer, of Lancaster, was born in 1659. He had two sons, Seth and Jonathan. Seth's descendants were Phineas, Caleb and John. Phineas married Hannah Whitcomb and had Seth and Abel. Seth had no issue. Abel had James, Phineas and Abel. James had Marshall. Caleb, son of Seth, married his second wife in 1766 and had Jonathan and Phineas. Jonathan had Caleb, Luke and

Augustus Jonathan. Caleb had Henry, Jonathan and Andrew. Luke had Wilbur Fisk, Wesley Caleb, Martin, John Priest, and Seth Augustus. Augustus Jonathan married Hannah Coolidge and had no issue. Phineas, second son of Caleb, had six sons, Wesley Jonathan — who had Charles, Frank Roswell and Fred — Francis Alfred, Edmund, and Zenas, who had one son, Walter. John, third son of Seth, had five daughters and no sons.

Jonathan, second son of Caleb, married Elizabeth Wheelock and had Mannasseh. Mannasseh married Lydia Fairbanks and had Jonathan (who died in the Revolution), Mannasseh, Jr., Luther and Jabez. Mannasseh had Mannasseh, Jr., Jonathan and Josiah. Luther, son of Jonathan, had Cephas, Arad, Nahum, Luther, Luke and Ached. Arad had Alfred and George.

John, sixth son of Thomas Sawyer, we cannot trace. He must have died before his father, as he is entirely ignored in the Will. Joseph Sawyer, son of Thomas, Jr., settled at " Sawyer's Mills," and married Abigail, daughter of John Beaman. He had four sons, Joseph, Jr., Thomas, Abner and Aaron. Joseph, Jr., married Tabathy Prescott. Joseph Sawyer, Sr., built the mills so long known as "Sawyer's Mills." At the death of Joseph, Sr., his widow had one run of mill-stones, with one-third of the water-power. Aaron had the other part of the grist mill, and Abner had the saw mill. Aaron Sawyer, Dr. Dunsmore, and Ephraim Sawyer, son of Nathaniel, were commissioned by the town of Lancaster to go to Boston and purchase cannon for the defence of the town. It was rainy weather and Aaron Sawyer took cold and had a fever, and died at the age of 43. He had two sons, Aaron, Jr., and Oliver. Aaron, Jr., became the owner of the whole mill, having bought out the right of his uncle Abner. He had three or four sons and three daughters. One of the daughters married Col. Hezekiah Gibbs, and was the mother of Gen. Aaron Sawyer Gibbs, now of Leominster, and Dolly S Gibbs who married Moses Wood. Oliver Sawyer married Patty Hinds and had a daughter, Patty Sawyer, who married Joshua Kendall; and was the mother of Oliver Sawyer Kendall. James, a law yer, son of Aaron, graduated from a college in Rhode Island, went to Texas and settled there and became wealthy. Abner, son of Aaron, died at 20 years of age. Joseph, the other son, was the father of Caleb, now of Clinton, and Ezra of Worcester. Two of the daughters married two brothers in Holden by the name of Howe, and one sister is living with Ezra Sawyer in Worcester.

Moses Sawyer, son of Joseph Sawyer, Jr., of Sawyer's Mills, and great-grandson of Thomas Sawyer, Jr., of Lancaster, settled in Lancaster, now Clinton. He had two wives ; the second wife was the sister of John Larkin, then of Lancaster, and afterwards of Berlin. She outlived her husband, and was 95 years of age at the time of her death. John Larkin settled Moses Sawyer's estate, and was a guardian for the three youngest children, who were daughters; their names were Luzena, Caty and Axey. Luzena married Ebenezer Wilder, and had three sons and one or two daughters. The sons I well knew ; their names were Ebenezer, Joseph and Sidney. The daughters I had seen, but did not know their names. Caty married Stephen Wilder and had several daughters and perhaps sons. The daughters I had seen, but knew not their names. Axey married Ephraim Hastings and had two children, a son and a daughter. The son's name was Moses Sawyer ; the daughter's name was Abigail. Ephraim Hastings settled in Berlin after the death of his first wife. He married the daughter of Rev. Reuben Puffer, of Berlin, and lived in the old Puffer mansion during the lifetime of Dr. Puffer's widow. He then purchased the place formerly owned by Nathan Johnson, of Revolutionary fame. He asserted that he stayed on Bunker Hill after all the rest had fled, and shot down three or four of the British, and said, " It made me mad to see the little cusses firing at me and could not hit me. I then went down the hill and came to a hogshead of toddy that had been made for the soldiers. It was all bloody from the wounds of the soldiers. There was nothing to drink out of, so I took off my old cocked hat and dipped up some and drank, and then put it on and followed after the rest."

Ephraim Hastings bought the estate and lived there till his death. His son, Christopher Sawyer Hastings, married a Miss Bigelow, of Marlborough, who was a descendant from John Bigelow who was associate prisoner with Thomas Sawyer, Jr., in Canada, and helped build the saw-mill, the price of which was their freedom.

This was a union of the descendants of the two Indian prisoners, one of whom came near being burned at the stake, and was only saved by the ruse of a Catholic Friar.

Christopher Sawyer Hastings settled with his father in Berlin. Abigail Hastings married the brother of the wife of C. S. Hastings; thus an even exchange between the towns, and, of course, no robbery. Both couples were descendants from the Canadian prisoners. The names of the sons of Moses Sawyer were Artemus, who graduated at Harvard College and was a lawyer; Peter, Ezra, and Joseph who died about the time of his father. Probably Ezra and Joseph were the two who were drowned in the pond. Peter had a son Peter who is now living in Clinton.

BOLTON SAWYERS.

The following statistics are from Joel Sawyer, of Bolton:

My grand father was William Sawyer, Jr., who was grandson of Thomas Sawyer, Jr., of Lancaster.

My great-grandfather, son of Thomas Sawyer, Jr., of Lancaster, settled in Bolton, then a part of Lancaster, and owned 300 acres of the excellent land lying south of the Bolton meeting-house. The old house, which was a block-house or what has been termed a garrison house, stood near the center of said tract of land, and remained there until about twenty years since, when it was taken down. He gave the land where the old burying-ground now is, situated on the old road from Bolton to Hudson. The remains of the said William Sawyer now lie in the ground which was his gift as a burying-field. The lands which he owned have principally remained in the hands of the Sawyer family, the principal farm being that of the late Joseph Sawyer. He was the principal progenitor of nearly all the Bolton and Berlin Sawyers. Deacon Josiah Sawyer, of Berlin, being the progenitor of the Berlin Sawyers, was one of the seven sons of William Sawyer, of Bolton, my grandfather being one of those sons. My father's name was Joseph; I had an uncle William, and uncles Josiah, Joseph, Benjamin, Barnabus and William. I had three brothers, Joseph, George, (myself named Joel) and Nathan. All of my brothers and sisters who had children have had grandchildren; and my brother Joseph, since his death, has had great-grandchildren. I have many cousins who have had children and grandchildren, but I cannot multiply names. Some of them went to Maine, but I cannot account for them. Their descendants are quite numerous and scattered about the country. My father was born one hundred and twenty-three years ago. He had a cousin in Templeton older than himself ; his name was Aholiab Sawyer ; he used to visit Bolton when I was a young man ; he married his wife here ; she was my wife's great-aunt. There are many generations descended from him in Templeton, but I do not think it of any use for you to go there, as it will take too much time to sift them down ; you have the regular line, and that will be sufficient.

Yours respectfully,

JOEL SAWYER.

BOLTON, MASS., March 12th, 1879.

A statement from William H. Sawyer, a descendant from the New Hampshire Sawyers:

WORCESTER, MASS., Feb. 6th, 1879.

My great-grandfather, whose name was John, was born about 1753, and lived when a boy in Hampsted, Mass., now part of Maine ; emigrated north to Salisbury, N. H., where he married a lady by the name of Couch ; had 4 sons and 5 daughters ; lived in Salisbury 20 years ; then moved to Lebanon, N. H., where he died.

My grandfather's name was John, born in 1789 ; two of his brothers went to Ohio, where their descendants now reside. My father's name is H. D. Sawyer.

Yours,

W. H. SAWYER.

A statement from Aaron Sawyer Gibbs, formerly of Boylston :

LEOMINSTER, MASS., April 11, '79.

AMORY CARTER, Esq —Sir :—I am a Sawyer on my mother's side ; was born in the town of Boylston, Oct. 20th, 1803. My grandfather was Aaron Sawyer, and my great-grandfather I do not know. I well remember my great-grandmother, who died in 1824, I believe ; but my great-grandfather died before my memory. My grandfather had a brother who settled in Boylston and had a family. My great-grandfather was the founder of the " Sawyer Mills " property in Boylston, and the old house is still standing, although altered within my memory. It was built in the year 1756. I do not certainly know the fact, but think his name was Aaron. His family was two sons and two daughters ; all married and had families. The daughters settled in Sterling, near the Sawyer Mills, and the two sons, Aaron and Oliver, settled in Boylston. Both had families, some of whom are still living. I am the oldest of the grandchildren of Aaron, and have a sister only, living in Worcester at No. 6 Allen Street, whose name was Dolly Sawyer Gibbs, now Woods.

I remember my grandfather, who died in April, 1817, aged about 66, it seems to me, but I am not positive about his age ; I am of the time of his death.

My grandmother Sawyer was a Richardson, and my great-grandmother Sawyer was a Moore   I cannot tell much more of my ancestors. I should be glad to know something of my great-grandfather's history. I think he was a man of considerable importance ; was a very large landholder, besides the founder of the Sawyer Mills. I know this by the dowry my great-grandmother had in real estate, which came to her from her husband. It has always been my impression that he came from Lancaster, but never knew. I have an impression that my great-grandmother Sawyer was buried in Sterling ; if so, it is probable my great-grandfather was also.

I do not know anything more of my ancestry than I have written, nor do I know who does. They are all gone. I am the oldest representative living. Hoping for the success of your undertaking, I am,

Respectfully yours,
AARON SAWYER GIBBS.

BOYLSTON SAWYERS.

RECORD OF THE SAWYER MILLS BRANCH.

The following record is from the pen of Oliver Sawyer Kendall, now deceased, the grandson of Oliver Sawyer, who was a descendant of Joseph Sawyer, the son of Thomas, Jr., of Lancaster. It was entrusted to me by said Kendall before his death, to be published in the Sawyer History. It is as follows, viz. : —

BOYLSTON, April 7th, 1879.

MR. CARTER.—*Dear Sir :* — Two months ago to-day you addressed a line to me, making inquiries respecting the branch of the Sawyer family that once lived in the town of Boylston, at and near the Sawyer Mills (so-called). It has been impossible for me to find one link of the succession of the Sawyer families. and only one, I think, from the present generation to the day Thomas Sawyer of Lancaster, made in his last will and testament on the sixth day of March, Anno Domini, 1705-6. There were five sons and one daughter named Mary, who married Mr. Wilder, of Marlborough. The names of the sons are as follows : Thomas, James, Joshua, Caleb and Nathaniel. This Thomas Sawyer being probably about eighty-three years of age at this date.

The wife of Thomas Sawyer was the daughter of John Prescott, and John Prescott was the son of Nathaniel Prescott, Sen., of Concord, in Middlesex County. May 18th, 1653. the name of Thomas Sawyer

EDITORIAL NOTE.—The widow of Thomas Sawyer was made executor of his Will, which will be seen in the following pages. Two of his sons, Ephraim and John, with Elizabeth, died before the Will was made. The names of the children in the Will are the same as here given.

appears with John Prescott, Ralph Houghton, Edward Burk, Nathaniel Hadlock and William Curley, as commissioners to lay out to the planters their lots, and assign to them their bounds within the town of Lancaster. In the Plymouth Colony Records it appears that on the third day of May, 1654, Thomas Sawyer took the oath of Freeman, with many others. The last Will and Testament of Thomas Sawyer, the second, of Lancaster, in the County of Middlesex, bearing date 26th day of August, A. D. one thousand seven hundred and nineteen, and in the fifth year of the reign of our Sovereign Lord, George, and King of Great Britain, Ireland and France. A part of his Will reads as follows, viz. : " I will and give unto my son Bezaleel Sawyer, and to his heirs and assigns forever, my mansion house, together with the whole living I now live upon and have possessed ever since the first Indian war; together with all that part of my stated Common which lyeth on the south-east side of the highway that goeth along before the house." There were two daughters ; Mary married Joshua Rice, and Hannah married Jonathan Moore, both of Marlborough ; and to these daughters a legacy was given, and the remainder of his estate was given to his four sons, William Sawyer, Joseph Sawyer, Bezaleel Sawyer, and Elias Sawyer, to be equally divided between these four, and to their heirs forever. William and Bezaleel were appointed executors of his Will.

It appears that this Thomas Sawyer and his son Elias, and Mr. Bigelow of Marlborough, were the men taken by the Indians and carried captive to Canada in 1705, and for their ransom they built a saw-mill (said to be the first saw-mill ever built in Canada), and then were detained for a time to learn the Canadians how to run their saw-mill. It appears that Joseph Sawyer, the second son of Thomas Sawyer, Jr., took up his place of residence near Sawyer's Mills, so called, in honor of the man. It appears, also, that Mr. John Beaman, Sen., a son of Bezeleel Beaman, gave to said Joseph Sawyer a Deed of a tract of land, lying on the Nashua River, which runs as follows : " Know you that I, John Beaman, Sen., of the town of Lancaster, in the County of Middlesex, in ye Province of the Massachusetts Bay, in New England, yeoman for and in consideration of ye Love and Respect which I have to my son-in-law, namely, Joseph Sawyer of Lancaster, aforesaid, Blacksmith; have granted and freely given, enforced, conveyed and confirmed, and by these presents for myself, my heirs, Executors &c -- do freely, fully, and absolutely give unto him, ye said Joseph Sawyer, the one half of my Lot and Right of Land lying in the new addition of land sometime purchased of George Tahonto and other Indians, and since confirmed by the Great and General Assembly of the Province aforesaid.'

The name of his wife was Abigail, and the names of their children

EDITORIAL NOTE.—There was a later Will made in 1735, which abrogates all other Wills. It is reorded in the Worcester County office. Why the former should have been recorded seems a mystery, unless it was recorded during the testator's life-time. A copy of the later Will will be seen in the following pages.

Joseph Sawyer, Thomas Sawyer, Abner Sawyer and three daughters.
Sarah married Ephraim Houghton. Asseneth married Jonathan Osgood,
and Mary married Thomas Sawyer. It appears that Thomas Sawyer 2d
owned a tract of land in the south part of Lancaster, on the Nashua
River, and his son Joseph became a resident and owner at or near what
is now called Sawyer's Mills. The deed of John Beaman to Joseph
Sawyer bears date the eleventh day of May, A. D 1721. The deed of
Sarah Taylor to Joseph Sawyer bears date of the 23d day of September,
A. D. 1723. Elizabeth Howe and others, of Marlborough, gave a deed
to "Joseph Sawyer, Blacksmith, of twenty-five and one half acres of
land that lieth on the Nashway River, and is the third Lot in Number on
the River in the second Division of Intervale, and on both sides of the
Nashway River." This deed was signed by Elizabeth Howe and six
others, partly of Marlborough and partly of Shrewsbury, and probably
came into their possessions in the settlement of the estate of Thomas
Sawyer the second, of Lancaster. This deed bears the date of " twenty-
second day of December A. D. one thousand seven hundred and twenty-
nine, and of the third year of Our Sovereign Lord, George the second,
of Great Britain, France, and Ireland, King."

I infer from the part of the several conveyances having been made
to Joseph Sawyer, Blacksmith, as early as 1721, May 12th, by John
Beaman, and six or seven other deeds given by other parties between
1721 and 1730, that the grist-mill or saw-mill could not have been built at
the Sawyer's Mills, previous to these dates, but probably a little later.
It appears by the Commissioners' Return to the Judge of Probate, John
Chandler, that they set to the widow, Abigail, in part for her thirds, one
half of the house, and one half of the barn, and one half of the corn-
mill, with the privilege of one third of the stream. It appears, also, that
Abner had one half the saw-mill set to him as part of his share of the
estate; and Joseph the eldest son had set to him one mill-stone and one-
third part of the mill stream, with land, and half of the house and barn.
The inference is that this Joseph Sawyer, son of Thomas Sawyer 2d, of
Lancaster, was the builder of the grist-mill and saw-mill at Sawyer's
Mills, some time between 1721 and 1751 or 1752,—which latter date must
have been about the time of his death, I think. On the 15th day of November, A. D. 1753, David Osgood, Esq., Asa Whitcomb, and George
Houghton, of said Lancaster, were appointed a committee to appraise
the widow Abigail Sawyer's dower,* and to divide among the proper
heirs of said Joseph 2d, deceased, according to law, by Hon. John Chand-

* Here seems to be a mistake. David Osgood, Asa Whitcomb and George
Houghton were appointed a committee to divide and set off to Abigail Beaman
Sawyer her thirds in her husband's (Joseph Sawyer, Senior,) estate. The record
says that Aaron, Jr , received a double portion, which, with a purchase of his Uncle
Abner's interest, gave him the whole mill, after his grandmother's death. According to the Kendall record, Abner was the son of Joseph, Sen. Thomas, Jr., deeded
property to his grandchildren, who were Joseph, Thomas, Abner and Aaron ; that
makes the family line correct, and O. Sawyer Kendall, of the seventh generation,

SECOND COLLATERAL BRANCH of CAMBRIDGE, MASS.

This memorandum I received some years ago from my
brother, Hon. Joel Swain Sawyer, of Minnesota, now deceased.
He obtained it at Cambridge, I believe, while on a visit to that
region. Elisha Sawyer, second son of Elias, lived on the old
homestead at Sterling, was three times married and had nine
children. His first wife's name was Bennett. His second Mary
Flagg, widow of Wm. Belknap. His third, Bowker. Children
by first wife, Paul; by second, William, Samuel Flagg, John,
Franklin and Elisha; by his third, Joán, Charles, and Louis.
Samuel Flagg, third son of Elisha, married Patience Leonard, of
Watertown, Mass., settled at Cambridge, and had seven children,
viz:—Samuel, Mary Ann, Louisa, Martha, Caroline, James and
Lucy. Mary married Jeremiah Browning, of Lawrenceburg, Ind.
Louisa married Wm. Thurston, of Newport, R. I. Martha mar-
ried Rev. H. Lawrence, of Ohio. Caroline died at the age of six
years. James and Lucy were at home at date of memorandum.
Dr. Samuel Sawyer, eldest son of Samuel Flagg Sawyer, married
Lucy Taft, of Charlestown, Mass., and had six children, whose
names I have not learned. The family lived at Cambridge, Mass.,
at date of memorandum.

This very hasty and rough letter, written during the pressure
of other important and official duties, concludes the information
in my possession relating to the members of the Sawyer family.
Laurentus T. Sawyer, of Watertown. N. Y., would be able to give
you more definite information in regard to his father's children
and descendants. Rev. Leicester A. Sawyer, of Whitestown, N.
Y., might give you further information relating to his brothers
and sisters, and their children. Dr. Cyrenus Wakefield, of Bloom-
ington, Ill., could give you further information in regard to his
brothers and sisters, and their families. Also, as to the several
sons of Elias Sawyer, who I have stated went to Illinois about
the time the Wakefields did, and into the same neighborhood.
Dr. Cyrenus Wakefield was a boy with me. He has become
wealthy; has travelled in Europe; has visited me in California,
and he now lives handsomely in an elegant house at Blooming-
ton, Ill. His business in the line of his medicines extends

through all the States of the Mississippi and Missouri valleys. Mrs. Lavina W. Sharp, of York, Nebraska, is an intelligent woman and could give you more particular information respecting her sister's families.

I do not know as there is anything more of interest to you relating to the Sawyer family within my reach. Hoping you may push your work to a successful and speedy completion.

I am respectfully yours,
LORENZO SAWYER.

[The following additional genealogy of the Watertown Sawyers has been furnished by Hon. Lorenzo Sawyer since the former article was written. He having recently discovered it.]

"Joseph Sawyer, born March 7, 1794, at Plymouth, Vt.; died Dec. 8, 1874. Mary Roper, his wife, born Oct. 21, 1797; died April 12, 1873. Married in November, 1818. Celebrated their Golden Wedding in November, 1868. Children of Joseph Sawyer and Mary :—Elvira M., born Aug. 22, 1820, died unmarried Aug. 20, 1843; Melissa E., born Aug. 8, 1822, died about 1850; Laurentus Thomas, born Nov. 25, 1824, lived on the homestead in Watertown, N. Y.; Mariette, born July 15, 1826, died May 6, 1881; Charlotte Maria, born June 19, 1830, died unmarried Nov. 10, 1851; Fanny Lucena, born Nov. 13, 1822; Joseph B., born June 16, 1838, died July 21, 1838.

Laurentus Thomas married Corrinne Tollman (born Sept. 13, 1830,) on Dec. 13, 1855. Children of Laurentus Thomas and Corrinne :—William Herbert, born Oct. 13, 1863; Frederick Laurentus, born July 18, 1872.

Fanny Lucena, married Geo. W. Hammond September 22, 1858. Children of George and Fanny :—Letta Sawyer, born July 10, 1860; William Fuller, born May 20, 1866; Annie Elizabeth, born Sept. 3, 1870.

Melissa married Dr. Wm. T. Clark about 1844, but died without children about 1850.

Marietta married Aaron Ormond Sawyer, a second cousin, on February 25, 1846. Aaron O., born May 16, 1814. Children of Ormond and Marietta :—Mary Melissa, born July 2, 1847;

Alice Elvira, born Aug. 23, 1848; Emily Lorrilla, born April 29, 1850; Joseph Ormond, born Feb. 6, 1852; Orville Day, born March 20, 1852; William Clark, born Oct. 11, 1855; Fannie Maria, born Nov. 14, 1857; Frank Fendes, born June 10, 1861, died Jan. 28, 1878; Cora May, born June 24, 1863.

Aaron Ormond Sawyer had before been married to Maria Lines, on June 19, 1836, by whom he had five children: Maria L., born Feb. 4, 1811, and died Sept. 20, 1844. Children of Maria L. and O.:—Sarah Maria, born Nov 30, 1837, died unmarried in 1846; Charles Samuel, born Oct. 7, 1839; Phebe Louise, born July 24, 1841, died Aug. 27, 1859; Henry Lines, born Jan 17, 1843, died Sept. 1, 1843; Harriet Rebecca, born July 1, 1844, died Sept. 23, 1844.

Charles Samuel,—first wife's son,—married Libbie Barney, April 15, 1862; had three children:—Freddie, Jennie and Florence. His wife, Libbie, died Nov. 8, 1879.

Alice E., daughter of Marietta and Ormond, married Albert V. Rogers, March 10, 1869, and have two children,—Emma M. and Annie M.

Emily Lavilla married Albert Sadden, Oct 22, 1873, and have two children,—Ormond H. and Florence M.

Joseph Ormond married Alice Johnson, Oct. 21, 1875, who died Nov. 20, 1879, when Ormond married Jennie Taylor, Aug. 10, 1880.

William C., married Libbie E. Cratsenburg, March 19.

Fannie M. married George Goodenough, March 1, 1875, and has three children:—Gertie O., Lomis J. and Margette.

Collateral to my branch is the following: Jotham Sawyer, the third son of Elisha, my grandfather's father, married the widow of Nathan Goodell, whose maiden name was Dinah Weeks, and had five children:—John, Dinah, Elizabeth, Jotham and Job, The last, Job, went to Watertown, N. Y., in the Spring of 1801, with his uncle, Thomas Sawyer, my grandfather, and settled on an adjoining tract of land, where he lived till he died. He married Rebecca Upham, and had two children:—Charlotte and Sylvia. Charlotte married John Dresser, and died without children. John Dresser then married Sylvia. Both are living, but are very aged and without children. Aaron Ormond Sawyer, whom I have already mentioned and given a list of his children, is a nephew of this Job, and a son of either John or Jotham, I am not certain which."

Although the emigrant Sawyers were from the farming class
of England, yet they were proverbially a race of mechanics.
Although they might be farmers they did not have to go to their
neighbors to procure a whip-staff, or a milking-stool, to be made.
They could arrange their own corn chambers, and make their
own potato bins. Their buildings did not go into dilapidation ;
they could nail on a board or a loose clap-board, or they could
patch a leaky roof. Said W. H. Sawyer, lumber dealer of Worcester: " I never knew a Sawyer who could not take care of
himself." If they were not born with saws in their hands, they
came readily to their hands afterwards. No class of people
could use them more precisely or dexterously. They were Mill-
Wrights, Wheel-Wrights, Carpenters, Coopers, Blacksmiths, Coppersmiths, Machinists, and Engineers ; also Shoe Makers and
Boot Manufacturers by the multitude.

I purpose here to speak of the Mill-Wrights, Mill Builders,
Mill owners and Manufacturers.

Thomas Sawyer, Jr., if not the master builder, was assistant
workman on the first corn mill ever built in Lancaster. It was
built either by his grandfather, John Prescott, or by his uncle,
John Prescott, Jr. It was situated in what is now Clinton, on
the site where the old cotton factory stood, during my boyhood,
which was owned by Plant & Poynard. It afterwards became a
Quilt Manufactory. Thomas Sawyer. Jr., built the first saw mill
ever built in Canada. In the copy of an old deed contained in
these pages he bound his son, Bezaleel, on land upon which he
built a mill. They first built their mills on small streams. The
first mill built on the Nashua River was probably that built in
Sawyers' Mills Village ; the old logs which were the basis of
that dam are probably now to be seen there as they were the
last time I saw it. I have been in the old mill that stood there,
and have seen the saw mill and the clothing mill, all of which
stood on the west side of the stream. The mill was probably
built by Thomas Sawyer, Jr., for his son Joseph. who was desig-

nated by John Beaman in a deed of gift made of the land on which
the pond and mill were situated, for the love he had for his son-
in-law, Joseph Sawyer, Blacksmith. Joseph Sawyer was the
owner of the mill, and it was built some time between the years
1728 and 1752, about which time Joseph Sawyer died. Very
probably Thomas Sawyer, Jr., was master builder of the mills
in South Lancaster, which were known in my boyhood as " Bennett's Mills," and were afterwards purchased by my uncle, and
were owned by him many years, and by his son afterwards. A
corn mill was burned down, and I was the master builder in erecting the present mill building that now stands upon the premises,
and also put in new timbers to the flume under the saw mill.
Another Thomas Sawyer succeeded Thomas Sawyer, Jr., in the
person of Thomas Sawyer of Bolton, who was a descendant of
Thomas Sawyer, Jr., of Lancaster. They probably built the first
corn mill ever built in Bolton, which was situated near the center
of the town. It is said the mill stones were six feet in diameter,
but they have since been cut down to smaller dimensions. In
the history of Winchendon it is stated that Thomas Sawyer of
Bolton built a mill at Jackson Pond in 1765, and the price is
given for doing the work as £24, 13s., and 6d. in full. He built
another mill on Otter River for his son Thomas, in 1762 or '63.
He also built the mills at Baldwinsville in 1767 or '68. He was
probably the Col. Thomas Sawyer mentioned in the *Vermont
Gazetteer*, who worked at mill building before the Revolutionary
War, and when the war broke out went immediately to the front,
and was chief constructor of the breast works on Bunker or
Breed's Hill. He afterwards commanded a military company at
Rutland, Vt., and was stationed at Tyconderoga after its capture
by Ethan Allen. He marched his company from Tyconderoga
to Rutland, in the midst of a severe snow storm, and some of
them becoming hungry and faint fell down and perished by the
way. He encouraged them on by telling them there was a house
ahead where he had ordered a warm supper. They struggled on
and found the house but no supper, which so warmed them with
anger that they reached Rutland in safety. After the war he
settled in Rutland. His mill-building propensities coming on he
went in search of a mill site and found it on the Leicester River,

what is now Salisbury. He built there a grist mill and saw mill, dressing out the mill-stones at Rutland with his own hands, put them on board a stone boat, and sent his son with an ox team to haul them through the wilderness, guided by marked trees and a compass. They arrived safely at their destination, and the mills were completed. The mill was supposed to be in Leicester, and he represented that town three years in the Legislature. He afterwards removed to Farmington, N. Y., where two years later he died. It is said a grandson of his now owns the mills and some of the timbers still remain where he placed them.

Thomas Sawyer, who is supposed to be the son of Colonel Thomas Sawyer, built the mills now standing on Waterquatic Brook, in the southern part of Bolton, recently known as Pollard's Mills;—Pollard being a son-in-law of Thomas Sawyer, and the mills having gone into his hands at Sawyer's decease. It is an excellent mill, as I know from personal knowledge, having been there frequently to procure grinding to be done, and noticed its structure and efficiency.

Another Sawyer mill stands down on the road leading from Bolton to Stowe, on what was known as the Pan, and was built, I think, by John Sawyer, and is now owned by his son, J. S. Sawyer. Another saw mill and mill-wright water power stands in the center of Bolton, and is owned by Joel Sawyer,—a Sawyer mill-wright of the present day. He began life as a watch maker, and I went to his shop several times in early life to get watch repairing done. He left watch making for mill building, and he once informed me that he had made wheels from an eighth of an inch to twelve feet in diameter. He is well known as a thorough mill-wright, and being 76 or 77 years of age is still a working mill-wright.

John Sawyer, who lived at Salisbury, twenty-one years afterwards, removed to Lebanon, N. H., and built the well known lumber mills there, which are now in possession of his descendants, and one of them,—W. H. Sawyer,—is now a lumber dealer in Worcester.

Phineas Sawyer, of Harvard, while working in a mill at Feltonville, now Hudson, Mass., was accidentally killed while cutting out a frozen water-wheel. Jonathan Sawyer, his son, built.

the Woolen Factory at Dover, N. H., and he and his sons now own and run those mills. They have what is known as the upper and lower mills, and are said to manufacture about a million dollars worth of goods yearly.

A. E. Sawyer, who was born in Templeton, Mass., is now a manufacturer of lumber at Leroy, Osceola county, Michigan, and is said to have one hundred and fifty men in his employ. All the above Sawyers were descendants of Thomas Sawyer of Lancaster.

Another, Philetus Sawyer, now U. S. Senator, a descendant of Caleb Sawyer, of Harvard, has, it is said, amassed a fortune of half a million dollars or more in the milling and lumber business at Minnesota,—all by his own personal merit and skill, having no aid, but the use of his head and hands.

There may be, and probably there are, other Sawyer millers whom I have not mentioned; but the above I know of and have dictated the descriptive, while sitting in my chair in blindness. Let any other race on this continent compare with it if they can.

I may be pardoned here for a little Autobiography. My mother was a Sawyer and I have some Sawyer proclivities. When I commenced life as a carpenter and builder, I built me a water-power with which to do my heavy work. I was master builder of the whole concern. I built the dam with the pilings and the flume. I helped cut all the timber from the stump, and hewed it all, and was master workman in framing the building, and in covering the same. I made the water-wheel, and only hired a mill-wright to hang it upon the shaft and letting the water upon it, for which I paid him twenty-four dollars. All the machinery I set up with my own hands. It consisted of two circular saws, a turning lathe, a planing machine, a turning machine, and a pair of grind-stones; all of which were in good running order. With these I made doors, sashes and blinds; and in the winter bedsteads, besides getting out all my inside finish for houses, and planing all my boards for floors; and that all before any other machinery for that purpose was established in Worcester county. I never served any apprenticeship, always having worked on a New England farm until I was twenty years of age, and I began work as a contracting builder at twenty-two years of age, and followed it forty-five years in succession, and until I had paralyzed my limbs by excessive labor, I could build a first class house and do every part of it,—the stone work, the carpenter work, painting, glazing, mason work of all kinds, and paper hanging : stair building, making doors, sashes, and blinds, piazzas, and colonades, entablatures, etc., always in all cases my own architect, drawing all my own plans, and never failing before any architect. I now live in a house made by my own hands, never having employed a mechanic or other workman on the premises : but by a sad accident I can do no more, nor see again what I have done. My greatest regret is that I can do no more to benefit the world and they that dwell therein. I said in early life the world should not be the poorer for my having lived in it, and I do not think it will if I live several years longer.

STERLING SAWYERS.

Nathaniel Sawyer, youngest son of Thomas, Sen., of Lancaster, was the first progenitor of the regular branch of Sterling Sawyers, as will be seen in the following record prepared by Dea. Samuel Sawyer, of Sterling, one of the fifth generation from Nathaniel Sawyer. It was contributed to me by his son, Luke Sawyer, Esq., who has since died. He informed me that his father spared no pains or expense to arrive at bottom facts. His record is the most perfect of any I have seen. I discover only one trivial error; it says that the three brothers were Edmund, William and Thomas. Savage's Genealogy is the best authority I can find. He finds Edmund Sawyer at Ipswich in 1636. He finds William at Salem, and Edward and Thomas at Rowley in 1643. The Rowley records substantiate the fact that there was in that town an Edward and Thomas Sawyer, each of them having had a lot of land set off to him, the boundary being given, one side of each being upon the ocean. This proves that Edward Sawyer of '43 was not Edmund Sawyer of '36. Edward Sawyer remained at Rowley, and Edmund Sawyer, about the year 1661, removed to York, which is now in Maine. Thomas Sawyer hearing of the purchase in the Nashua Valley by Thomas King, repaired to Watertown, saw King and went thence to the Nashua Valley, and remained there until the day of his death, in 1706, aged 90 years. William Sawyer went to Newbury in 1645. Thus it is proved that Edmund Sawyer was not one of the three brothers. I know of no other mistake in the Dea. Samuel Sawyer record.

A RECORD OF THE SAWYERS, MADE BY SAMUEL SAWYER OF

STERLING, MASS., SON OF EZRA AND MARTHA SAWYER,

OF STERLING.

Edmund, William and Thomas Sawyer, brothers, came to this country in 1635 or 1636. They came passengers with one Capt. Parker and were from Lincolnshire, England.

Edmund settled in Ipswich in 1636.—*See Felt's History of Ipswich.*

William settled in Newbury, now Newburyport, in 1645.—. *See Farmer's Genealogical Register.*

William settled in Lancaster in 1647 or 1648.—*See Willard's History of Lancaster and also the records of Lancaster.*

He was one of the first four who subscribed to a covenant entered into, for themselves, heirs, etc.—*See said History, Worcester Magazine, pages* 278 *and* 279.

Thomas Sawyer's garrison was in that part of Lancaster known by the name of New Boston, and a little north of the house of John G. Thurston, Esq., formerly Samuel Flagg's.— *See Willard's History of Lancaster, page* 300 *of Worcester Magazine.**

The Sawyers in Lancaster, Sterling and Bolton, are descendants of Thomas Sawyer.

---

*NOTE.—Thomas Sawyer's garrison was on the east side of the road, in what is now Main Street, South Lancaster, as is proven by a deed given by Thomas Sawyer, Sen., to his son Nathaniel in 1689. One item of conveyance was ten acres of the homestead, which was bounded on the north by the remaining homestead, and on the east and west by town roads, and on the south by a lane. That fixes the homestead, positively, on the east side of the old town road in South Lancaster. That deed also fixes the fact that one of the two children of Thomas Sawyer, said to have died in childhood, must have lived until early womanhood, as a life right in that deed was reserved for Hannah if she needed it, and she must have been eighteen or twenty years of age at that time. The other two daughters' names were Mary and Elizabeth. Thus there were three daughters and seven sons who arrived at mature age.

Thomas, one of the first settlers of Lancaster, and Mary, his wife, had nine children:—*Thomas, born July, 1649; †Ephraim, born Jan., 1651, N. S.; Mary, born Jan., 1653, N. O.; Elizabeth, born Jan., 1654; Joshua, born March, 1655; James, born March, 1657; Caleb, born April, 1659; John, born April, 1661; Nathaniel, born Nov., 1670.—*Worcester Magazine, page* 298. *See Willard's History of Lancaster.*

Thomas, eldest son of the first Thomas, was born July, 1649. The name of his wife was Mary. They had six children whose names are found in his will: Bezaleel, Mary, who married a Rice, Hannah, who married a Moore, William, Joseph and Elias.

Nathaniel, the youngest son of the first Thomas, was my father's great grandfather, and was born Nov., 1670. He had ten children:—Samuel, born 1697, Amos, Ezra, born 1702, Thomas, born 1711, Ephraim, John, Phineas, Nathaniel, Jonathan, and Eunice, who married a Gates.

Samuel, son of Nathaniel of Lancaster, was one of the first settlers of Sterling; (*see Goodwin's History of Sterling, Worcester Magazine, page* 39). His farm is now owned, in 1850, and occupied by a great grandson of his. It is situated on a hill about two miles from Sterling Meeting House.

Amos lived in Lancaster. I know but little of him.

Ezra settled in the east part of Sterling, one-fourth of a mile south of the Redstone School House, on the farm lately owned by Moses Thomas, Esq.

Ephraim settled a little east of said school house on the farm now owned by the Widow Powers.

Thomas settled west of the West Washacum Pond.

John settled in the north-east part of Sterling, but left town and went to the West.

Samuel was born in 1697. He married Deborah Rugg, of Lancaster. They had eight children:—Mary married J. Kilburn; Azubah married Nathan Burpee; Samuel, born Jan. 2, 1740, O. S.; Lucy married a Brooks; Deborah married Jonas Wilder; Betsey married Silas Wilder; Joshua married Esther Jewett; Ruth married David Jewett.

*On the 15th of October, 1705, Thomas Sawyer, his son Elias and John Bigelow were taken captives by the Indians and carried to Canada.

†Ephraim was killed by Indians at Prescott's Garrison, Feb., 1676.

Capt. Samuel Sawyer married Phœbe Cooper, daughter of Moses Cooper. They had nine children:—Cooper, born Nov. 14, 1768, died, Oct., 1830 ; Samuel, born Oct. 11, 1770, died Nov., 1848 ; Martha, born Oct. 30. 1772, died March, 1853 ; Phœbe, born Sept. 1, 1774, died July, 1793 ; Putman born Aug. 23, 1776, died Oct., 1843 ; Ruth, born Nov. 11. 1778, died Oct.. 1857 ; Mary, born Nov. 10, 1781, died March, 1864 : Moses, born April 27, 1784, died Jan., 1870 ; Sally, born Feb. 14, 1786, died March, 1792.

Ezra Sawyer, son of Nathaniel of Lancaster, born 1702, married Rebecca Whitcomb. They had eight children:—Prudence, born Sept. 1, 1726 ; Elizabeth, born July 2, 1728 : Ezra, born Aug. 18, 1730 ; Rebecca, born Feb. 14, 1736 : Keziah, born May 9, 1737 ; Esther, born May 5, 1739 ; Nathaniel, born March 1, 1741, died young ; Major Menassah. Prudence married Joseph House ; Elizabeth married a Richardson ; Rebecca married Levi Moore of Boylston ; Keziah married John May ; Esther married Josiah Kendall : Nathaniel died young ; Menassah married Lucy Richardson.

Ezra married Keziah Sawyer, daughter of Abner and Mary Sawyer. They had four children:—Abner, born Nov. 3, 1762 ; Ezra, born March 20, 1764 : Thomas, born April 15, 1766 : Nathaniel, born Sept. 10, 1769.

Capt. Ezra, my grandfather, lived in Sterling and owned the farm I now own ; he had the command of a company of soldiers at the commencement of the Revolution, and went to Dorchester to join the army, and was taken sick and died suddenly. His remains were brought to Sterling and his grave is a few rods south of the gate in the old part of the Burying Ground in Sterling. After the death of Capt. Ezra his wife married Ephraim Powers, and they had two children :—Keziah married H. Wilder, and Ephraim married Betsy Kimball.

Abner was a soldier in the army of the Revolution when only 16 years old, and the hardships of the camp were too fatigueing for his slender constitution. He was taken sick and died at Albany.

Capt. Ezra was my father. He went to the State of New York when young, and purchased a tract of land on the Mohawk

River, and resided there two or three years, and then sold it and returned to the homestead of his father, which he and his brother Thomas owned, and with the addition of a part of the Seaver farm they made two very good farms. Ezra Sawyer died Feb. 1, 1828. His wife, Martha Sawyer, died March 1, 1853.

Nathaniel, born Sept. 10, 1768, never married. He died March, 1835.

Thomas Sawyer, son of Ezra and Keziah Sawyer, married Elizabeth Houghton, Jan. 8, 1789. He was born April 15, 1766. He died Aug. 16, 1825. His wife, Elizabeth, was born Jan. 1, 1769, and died May 16, 1856.

Ezra, son of Ezra and Keziah, married Martha Sawyer, daughter of Samuel and Phœbe Sawyer. Ezra and Martha Sawyer had three children :—Samuel, born Nov. 13, 1800 ; Ezra, Jr., born Feb. 20, 1804 ; Martha, born Jan. 28, 1808.

·Ezra Sawyer, Jr., son of Ezra and Martha, died Oct. 4, 1806.

Martha Sawyer married Augustus G. Hill, of Harvard, Jan. 15, 1837, and died July 31, 1837.

Samuel Sawyer, son of Ezra and Martha, married Eunice Houghton Nov. 20, 1823. They had five children :—Jane E., born Dec. 15, 1824 ; Ezra, born April 8, 1827 ; Fred A., born April 4, 1832; Mary, born Jan. 20, 1834 : Henry S., born July 15, 1843.

Jane E. married Geo. Goss, Oct. 18, 1855.

Fred. A. married, July 29, 1855, Helen M., daughter of Christopher Deane, M. D., of Coleraine. They had four children :—Fred. D., born Sept. 8, 1857 ; Sarah H., born Aug. 12, 1859; Charles P., born Aug. 6, 1862 ; Fanny A., born April 23, 1867.

Ezra Sawyer, born April 8, 1827, lives on the old homestead (1879). In 1862 he joined the army and started the 18th of Jan. from New York on board the steamer *Continental*, and was detailed clerk to acting Brig. General Gooding. Ezra belonged to the 53d Regiment, Massachusetts Volunteers. He went to New Orleans. The regiment arrived in Fitchburg Aug. 24, 1863.

Dr. Fred. A. Sawyer started from New York Tuesday, Dec. 2, 1862, on board the steamer *Illinois*, one of General Banks' fleet, for New Orleans, surgeon of the 51st Regiment, Massachusetts Volunteers. He arrived at New Orleans Dec. 14, and at Baton Rouge Dec 17.

Henry S. married, Oct. 3, 1866, Mary L. Burpee, daughter of James and Eunice Burpee. They had four children :—Arthur H., born July 19, 1868 ; Mabel Jane, born Dec. 19, 1870 ; Ezra Warren, born Dec. 17, 1872 ; Elsie Eunice.

Thomas, son of Ezra and Keziah Sawyer, married Elizabeth Houghton, Jan. 8, 1789. They had eight children :—Ezra, born July 22, 1794 ; Thomas, Jr., born Oct., 18, 1796 ; Amey, born April 25, 1799 ; Luke, (died young,) born Aug. 19, 1801 ; Susan, born Sept. 20, 1802 ; Mary E., born March 22. 1806 ; Nathaniel, born Sept. 2, 1808 : Luke, born Jan 23, 1814.

Ezra married Eliza Houghton, of Lancaster, Feb. 7, 1821. They had seven children :—Edmund H., born Nov. 16, 1821 ; Henry H., born April 18, 1824 ; Ezra T., born Jan. 4, 1827 ; Francis O., born July 30, 1829 ; Nathaniel C., born Aug. 15, 1831 ; Sarah E., born Aug. 7, 1835 ; Eliza A., born Dec. 31, 1839.

Thomas, Jr., married Polly Wright, July 4, 1819. They had four children :—Mary C., born May 13, 1820 ; Martha W., born Oct. 20, 1825 ; Elizabeth E., born Jan., 1828 ; Emory T., born March. 1835.

Amey married John D Pratt, June 3, 1823. They had eight children :—Mary E., born June 13, 1825 ; Sarah G., born Aug. 4, 1826 ; Harriett P., born Oct. 19, 1828 ; Henry T., born Dec. 1, 1829 ; Charles E., born Dec. 28, 1833 ; Harriett P., born Aug. 20, 1836 ; John L., born Dec. 31, 1839 ; Emma F., born Aug. 30, 1842.

Mary married Columbus Tyler, March 31, 1835.

Nathaniel married Emily Clark, March 15, 1847. They had four children :—Henry N., born Feb. 11, 1848 ; Mary E., born Aug. 28, 1850 ; Joseph, born Dec. 7, 1852 ; Edmund, born July 6, 1856.

Luke married Martha Burpee, May 1, 1844. They had five children :—Henry F., born Feb. 15, 1845 ; Christopher T., born Aug. 23. 1848 ; Anna E., born Sept. 30, 1850 ; Charles A., born Sept 6, 1855 ; Martha C., born Oct. 29, 1857.

Ephraim Sawyer was the father of Abner as near as we can make out, son of Nathaniel.

Abner and Mary were the parents of Keziah; who married Ezra Sawyer. They had five children :—Hannah married a Butterick; Keziah married Ezra Sawyer; Relief married Richard Rand; Mary married a Houghton; Prudence married a Randall of Stowe.

Abner Sawyer owned the Capt. Silas Howe place more than one hundred years ago. Mary, his wife, died at the place where he now lives; she came to live with Keziah, her daughter, on her son-in-law, Ezra's, place.

EDMUND HOUGHTON SAWYER.

[From the Hampshire Gazette.]

"Edmund Houghton Sawyer was born in Newton, Mass., Nov. 16, 1821, and had just passed his 58th year at the time of his decease. His father was Ezra Sawyer, who was the fifth in the regular line of descent from Thomas Sawyer, who came from England in 1647, and was one of the first six settlers of Lancaster, Mass. His mother was Eliza Houghton, of Lancaster, who was a descendant of Ralph Houghton, one of these first six settlers. His father was born in Sterling and his mother in Lancaster, both in 1794. Ezra Sawyer was a prominent master mason, and built the State Asylum at Utica, N. Y., and the Bigelow Carpet Mill, the Clinton Co.'s Mill, and the Lancaster Mills, at Clinton, the latter being among the largest mills in the country. He was a member of the Legislature, and otherwise prominent in public affairs. Edmund received such early education as the schools of Lancaster afforded, and subsequently attended the Derby Academy at Hingham. He early developed such qualities as gave promise of usefulness in the management of business affairs, and in 1836, at the age of 15 years, he entered the large mercantile establishment of Abraham Holman, of Bolton. Here he remained five years, and rose from the position of "boy-of-all-work" to be the chief clerk in the establishment. At 20 years of age he left Bolton, and after spending a few months in the vicinity of Boston, went to Brattleboro', Vt., and became clerk in the wholesale and retail hardware, drug and grocery store of Williston & Tyler, where he remained eight years. Here his business abilities continued to develop. Mr. Nathan B. Williston of this firm, was one of the three noted sons of Rev. Payson Williston of Easthampton, and through his recommendation young Sawyer was introduced to the notice of Samuel Williston, who was then just entering upon that great period of prosperity which gave him his ample fortune. Mr. Williston had recently begun the manufacture and sale of woven elastic rubber goods. He took Mr. Sawyer into his employ and gave him his confidence, and to the day of his death he retained him as his trusted friend and confidential adviser. Mr. Williston was a man of great foresight and power to read men and measure their capacities, and Mr. Sawyer, though coming to him as he did in the freshness of his early manhood and without much experience, justified his expectations and retained his confidence without a break for a full quarter of a century.

In 1850, the Nashawannuck Manufacturing Company was organized for the manufacture of elastic fabrics, with a capital of $100,000, afterwards increased to $300,000. Mr. Sawyer was chosen its first treasurer and general agent, also one of the directors, and these positions he held from that time to the day of his death. It was in the discharge of the duties of these offices that he displayed those rare business abilities which placed him in the front rank of successful manufacturers. Under his management the company enjoyed a remarkable degree of prosperity, and was never in better condition than it is at the present time.

Mr. Sawyer was actively interested in many other business enterprises in Easthampton. He was a director in the Easthampton Rubber Thread Co., the Easthampton Gas Co., and the Williston Mills, being also treasurer and general agent of the latter establishment from 1871 to 1875. He was also director, president for a short time, and treasurer of the Glendale Elastic

Fabrics Company. The trust which Mr. Williston reposed in Mr. Sawyer was shown by his calling him, in 1871, to assist him in extricating the Williston Mills from what seemed a disastrous condition. Under bad management these mills had been losing money at the rate of $100,000 a year, and Mr. Williston was in great trouble and perplexity ; but in two years after Mr. Sawyer assumed the control, they were rescued from disaster and placed upon a sound foundation. Mr. Williston further manifested his confidence in Mr Sawyer by making him one of the executors of his will, and upon him, as principal resident executor, fell the bulk of the work of settling that large estate. This has been nearly accomplished, and a handsome gain has been realized on the inventory taken soon after the death of Mr. Williston in 1874.

Mr. Sawyer was prominent and active in the organization of the First National Bank of Easthampton, and was one of the directors from the first. He was also for many years a director of the First National Bank of Northampton, and president and trustee of the Easthampton Savings Bank. He was a trustee of the State Lunatic Hospital at Northampton from 1864 to the time of his death ; a trustee of Mt. Holyoke Female Seminary at South Hadley since 1873 ; a trustee of Williston Seminary since 1867, and for several years past was treasurer of the same. In 1859 and again in 1861, he visited Europe on business for the companies he represented. In 1878, the degree of Master of Arts (A. M.) was conferred upon him by Amherst College.

Mr. Sawyer has ever manifested a lively interest in the welfare of Easthampton, and there has seldom been, during his residence in the town, an enterprise designed for the promotion of the public good with which he has not been actively identified. He was the original mover in the establishment of the Public Library Association, and gave toward its establishment $1,000, Mr. Williston contributing $1,000 more at his solicitation. Since the establishment of the Library, he has given unsparingly of his time and efforts for its advancement, and has further shown his interest in it by giving it a legacy of $5,000.

Of public offices he has held many. He has been a Justice of the Peace for many years, and a Notary Public since 1864. He has often served as moderator of town meetings, and his

11

voice was frequently heard there in advocacy of enterprises for the advancement of the public welfare. He took an active part in the work of village improvement, and was a leading member of the society formed for that purpose. In this department his good taste as well as his excellent judgment found a fruitful field for their exercise. He did much towards enlarging and beautifying the cemeteries in town. He was foremost in the work of erecting the chapel in the upper factory village. Politically he was a Republican, earnest and true : was active and unfaltering during the rebellion in raising troops and otherwise supporting the government : and in 1874 took a leading part in the independent movement which resulted in the election of Prof. Seeley to Congress. In 1867 he represented the First Hampshire District in the House of Representatives, and in 1868 and 1869 was Senator for Hampshire County. While in the Senate, he proposed and advocated several measures of local interest and value, among them the donation of state aid to the Mt. Holyoke Female Seminary, a measure which was warmly appreciated by the friends of that institution.

Mr. Sawyer was also active in all religious and social matters, and in these departments manifested the same lively interest that characterized his conduct of business affairs. He was a member of the Payson Church and Society from its organization, and for twelve years was one of the deacons. He also served as superintendent of the Sunday School, and leader of the choir, of which he was an active member for thirty years. Socially he was a born leader. His house was always open for meetings of the church and society. He gave liberally to charitable objects, and to the needy, and he will be missed by the poor, for whom he did much. During the recent protracted depression in business he made special efforts to keep the mills in operation, so that the poor people could have employment and earn a living.

In other ways, Mr. Sawyer was also useful to his fellow-citizens. He was often consulted by them in regard to business matters and troubles and perplexities of various kinds, and freely gave his assistance. His judgment in regard to investments was often sought, and always proved beneficial to those who accepted it.

This is indeed a remarkable record for a man still in the prime of life. Few men in an existence of four-score and ten years attain such prominence, or accomplish as much, and it is widely recognized as a great public loss that a man so capable and so useful should be taken away at so early an age. The loss of men of great usefulness at an advanced age usually occasions no shock to the public, because their decease is expected, and in a measure is provided for in advance ; but when men are suddenly taken from the active discharge of their duties, in the midst of their most vigorous years, when ripeness of judgment gives them a power and an influence which is only attained in mature life, there is a shock. It is so in this case. A man is gone whose loss will be keenly felt. He is taken away in the midst of his greatest usefulness and when it seems as if he could not be spared.

Though filling so many important positions of trust and responsibility, and in a manner noteworthy for its general, and, it may be truly said, universal, acceptability. Mr. Sawyer was withal a man of singular modesty. He never obtruded himself upon public or private attention, nor sought notoriety for the distinction it gave. His mind was of a philosophical cast. When he had done what his judgment and his conscience dictated, he was content to rest and abide the result. He was a man of system, and method ruled all his labors. This was one of the chief reasons why he was able to accomplish so much in so short a time. He was a conscientious man, and acted from principle. He was a deeply religious man, and recognized the authority of the great Ruler in all human affairs. He was generous, kind-hearted, of tender sensibilities, and noted for his hospitality. His home was free to all. He was unselfish, of amiable disposition, void of harshness, loved to do deeds of kindness, and no man ever forgave more freely the unkind acts of others, or could more speedily obliterate from his memory the sense of wrong. He was a good neighbor, as well as a good citizen. He won friends, and held them. He formed strong attachments, and preserved them. His was a rare combination of the desirable qualities in human character. Few men are so well balanced, so self-poised, so admirably qualified to mould and lead the people in

right ways. Physically he was of slight build, and did not pass
for a marked man among strangers. He was retiring and gentle
in demeanor; he ever wore a smile, his voice was winning, and
his face gave evidence of his gentleness of spirit and kindness of
heart. Some men are leaders by force of will, are bold, coura-
geous, aggressive Others, no less successful, are leaders by
virtue of their gentleness and persuasiveness, combined with apt-
ness and superior judgment. Of this class was Mr. Sawyer. He
was a leader. He exerted great influence, and the whole community will miss him, and mourn as for the loss of a friend and
helper.

Among the things in contemplation by Mr. Sawyer previous
to his death, was the preparation of a sketch of the Nashawannuck Company from its organization to the present time, showing
its rise, progress, and present condition. This he designed to
have read at the annual stockholders' meeting on Dec. 17th: and
at the same time he proposed to ask for a leave of absence for
several months, with a view to the recovery of his health.

As the intelligence of his serious illness and death spread
abroad, much public sorrow was expressed, and many letters and
messages of sympathy and condolence have been received by the
family. Ex-Gov. Bullock, of Worcester, wrote on the morning
of his decease, expressing his deep personal interest in the welfare of his friend, and the hope that he would soon recover his
former health and cheerfulness. Writing after his decease he
says :—' I recur now with deep melancholy to the pleasant and
intimate acquaintance I was privileged to have with him, which
inspires my profound respect and esteem for all his amiable qualities and for his whole character. The memory of that character,
developed by religious principles and ornamented by every social
and personal trait worthy of a Christian gentleman, will constitute
for you a solace amid your grief.' Senator Dawes writes:—
' Every hour of my acquaintance with Mr. Sawyer has been filled
with his cordiality and kindness, but the last few hours at your
house so recently will be associated in my memory with a gentleness and tenderness which now seem hardly to belong to this
world.' Frederick Billings, of Vermont, President of the Northern Pacific R. R. Co., telegraphs his sympathy, and says :—' How

can such a good man, so genuine and faithful and true in every relation in life, be spared? Every good man and every good cause will mourn.' B. D. Harris, of Brattleboro', in a letter to a mutual friend, estimates him as ' A man, take him all in all, conspicuous among ten thousand for his sterling integrity and manly virtues.'

In his domestic relations, Mr. Sawyer was especially happy. He loved his home and his family, and did everything for them which ample means and a generous heart could devise and execute. Eighteen years ago he erected a large and commodious house on a beautiful lot of twelve acres south of the village, and fitted it up with every comfort and convenience. The grounds are laid out with excellent taste, Mr. Sawyer taking especial pleasure in the arrangement of lawn and shrubbery. His appreciation of art was remarkable. He keenly enjoyed good music, and from early manhood sung in the church choir. Only a few weeks before his decease, and the last time his sweet tenor was heard on earth, he joined with his three sons in completing the harmony of a glee. The occasion to them is now most memorable. He read much and his library was stocked with the works of standard authors, such as are delighted in by professional men and scholars. The paintings of Bierstadt, Hart, De Haas, Bricher, and those of other artists that at present ornament the walls of his home, evince the pleasure he took in all works of art.

He was twice married—first at Brattleboro', in 1848, to Mary A. Farnsworth, by whom he had one son, Henry H., who graduated at Williston Seminary and Amherst College, and since May, 1875, has been associated in business with his father, as secretary of the Nashawannuck Company. His second marriage was in 1853, to Sarah J. Hinckley, of Norwich, N. Y. Their family consists of three children: William B., a graduate of Williston Seminary, Amherst College, and Harvard Medical School, and a resident physician; Edmund H., a student in Williston Seminary; and Mary, now attending Miss Burnham's school at Northampton.

DESCENDANTS OF NATHANIEL SAWYER, JR.,

Grandson of Thomas Sawyer of Lancaster. Contributed by WARREN SAWYER, ESQ., *President of the Everett National Bank of Boston, who is a descendant of said Nathaniel Sawyer.*

Thomas Sawyer (the emigrant) married Mary *Prescott*.
Their children were:

Thomas, b. July, 1649; m. 1st, Sarah, 1670, 2d, Hannah, 1672, and 3d, Mary White, 1718, *Levins*

Ephraim, b. Jan. 26, 1651; killed at Prescott's Garrison by Indians, 1675.

Mary, b. Jan. 14, 1653; m. Nathaniel Wilder.

Joshua, b. March 16, 1656; m. Sarah Potter.

James, b. April 1, 1658: settled in Pomfret, Conn.

Caleb, b. April 1, 1659; m. Sarah Houghton.

John, b. April, 1661; m. Mary Ball in 1686.

Elizabeth, b. Jan., 1663: m. James Hosmer.

Deborah, b. ——; died in infancy, July, 1666.

Nathaniel, b. Dec. 4, 1670; m., 1st, Mary, and 2d, Elizabeth.

Martha, b. Aug., 1673.

Nathaniel Sawyer, born Dec., 1670; married, 1st, Mary, 2d, Elizabeth. Their children were:

Amos, b. June, 1693; m. Abigail Houghton.

Nathaniel, b. ——; m. Mary Houghton.

Ephraim, b. ——; m. Sarah.-

Ezra, b. ——, 1702; m. Rebecca Whitcomb.

John, b. ——.

Samuel, b. ——, 1698; m. Deborah Rugg; d. in 1784.

Manassah, b. ——.

Thomas, b. ——, 1711; d. July, 1787—buried in Sterling. ——

Phineas, b. ——.

Eunice, b. ——; m. —— Gates.

Nathaniel Sawyer, born ——; married —— Mary Houghton. Their children were;

Oliver, b. July, 1735; d. young.

Mary, b. Jan., 1737: m. —— Carter.

Elizabeth, b. July, 1741; d. in infancy.

Elizabeth, b. July, 1742; m. Levi Nichols.

Nathaniel. b. Feb., 1744; m. Catherine Ellis.

Thankful, b. Oct. 8, 1752; m., 1st, —— Clark, 2d,—— Houghton.

Jonathan, b. ——; slain by Indians.

Nathaniel Sawyer, born Feb. 21, 1744; married Catherine Ellis, born Sept. 28, 1748. Their children were:

Oliver, b. May, 1772; m. Mary Wilder.

Dolly, b. Nov. 8, 1773; m. Josiah Whitcomb.

Mary, b. Nov. 12, 1775; m. Cyrus Daniels.

Jonathan, b. March, 1778; m. Mary Crane Wild in 1819.

Nathaniel, b. Jan. 8, 1780.

Catherine, b. March, 1782: m. Elijah Hill.

Cynthia, b. March, 178-; m., 1st, Eben Wheelock, 2d, Asa Whiting.

Alpheus, b. June, 1786; m. Elizabeth Damon.

John, b. Oct., 1788; settled in Vermont.

Jonathan Sawyer, born March, 1778, in Sterling, Mass.; married Mary Crane Wild, born Nov., 1796, in Braintree, Mass. They were married in Boston, Mass. Their children were:

George, b. July 26, 1822; m., 1st, Susan Eames, 2d, Lois.

Warren, b. May 23, 1825; m., 1st, Mary E. Fuller, 2d, R. Alphia Fuller, 3d, E. R. White.

Mary Elizabeth, b. Sept, 1825; m. Jonathan R. Perkins.

Warren Sawyer, born May 23, 1825, in Boston, Mass.; m. Mary E. Fuller, born July 26, 1826, died Aug. 30, 1852: Rachel Aphia Fuller, born July 28, 1824. died Oct. 14, 1872; Ellen Reed White, born Oct. 22, 1843. Their children were:

Fanny Fuller, b. Oct. 15, 1851.

Herbert, b. Nov. 26, 1855.

Mary Cummings, b. March 28, 1864.

Warren Sawyer is the son of Jonathan Sawyer and Mary Crane Wild, who was the son of Nathaniel Sawyer and Catherine Ellis, who was the son of Nathaniel Sawyer and Mary Houghton. who was the son of Nathaniel, who was the son of Thomas, sen., the emigrant.

NOTE.—Jonathan Sawyer died in Medford, Mass., in August, 1831, and buried in Boston.

88

The following record of JOSHUA SAWYER, fourth son of Thomas Sawyer of Lancaster, is from Timothy T. Sawyer, Esq , of Charlestown, who is president of a Savings Bank in Charlestown and member of the Boston Board of Water Works, and is himself a descendant from Joshua Sawyer:

Joshua, born ———; died July 14, 1738: married Sarah ——. Their children were:
Abigail, b. 17 of 3 mo., 1679.
Joshua, b. June 4, 1684; m. Mary Carter, May 22, 1706.——
Sarah, b. July 4, 1687.
Hannah, b. Nov. 28, 1689.
Martha, b. April 26, 1692.
Elizabeth, b. Nov. 1, 1698.

Joshua, born June 4, 1684; died March 1, 1738; married Mary Carter, Oct. 5, 1685; d. Oct. 23, 1751. Their children were:
Mary, b. Sept. 14, 1706; m. Stephen Richardson.
Ruth, b. March 6, 1709.
Sarah, b. Sept. 13, 1711.
Joshua, b. May 5, 1713; m. K. Richardson.
Abigail, b. Nov. 8, 1714; m. John Childs, 1754.
John, b. Aug. 31, 1716; m. Abigail Thompson.
James, b. June 22, 1718.
Phœbe, b. Jan. 3, 1720; m. Samuel Tidd.
Benjamin, b. Nov. 24, 1721. ——
Oliver, b. July 19, 1726; m. Sarah Bowditch.
Jonathan, b. July 19, 1728; m Elizabeth Tenney. ——

Oliver, born July 19, 1726; married Sarah Bowditch. Their children were:
Oliver, b Jan. 31, 1752; d. in infancy, Sept 15, 1752.
Oliver, b. Feb. 8, 1753; d. in infancy, Sept. 28, 1754.
William, b. Sept. 20, 1754; m., 1st, Hannah Snow, 2d, Widow Hannah Snow, 3d, Widow Bethiah W. Wyman.
Oliver, b. Sept. 12, 1757.
Sarah, b. April 24, 1760; m. —— Nichols.
Hannah, b. July 14, 1761; married and moved into New Hampshire.
Timothy, b. Jan. 8, 1763.

William, born Sept. 20, 1754; died July 1, 1817 ; Hannah Snow, born —— ; died Jan. 14, 1790 ; Hannah Snow, widow, born —— ; died Dec. 1, 1806. The children were all by the first wife as follows, and were born in Haverhill :

Peter, b. Nov. 17, 1780 ; m. Charlotte Chickering of Charlestown, 1809.

Susannah, b. Dec. 4, 1781 ; d. in infancy.

William, b. March 3, 1783 ; m. Susannah Thompson of Charlestown, 1807.

Susannah, b. May 17, 1784 ; d. Feb., 1827.

Betsey, b. May 24, 1785 ; m. John Pierce. .

Leonard, b. Jan. 12. 1787 ; m. Abigail Brickett of Haverhill.

Hannah, b. Oct. 5, 1788 ; m. William How of Haverhill.

William, born March 3, 1873 ; died May 1, 1830 ; married Susannah Thompson, born March 24, 1791 ; still living. Children as follows :

William, b. Dec. 15, 1807 ; d. May 24, 1852 ; m. Susan M. Gibbs, of Charlestown.

Susan L., b. Sept. 12, 1809.

Mary T., b. March 3, 1812 ; d. March 25, 1860.

Harriett E., b. Sept. 29, 1814 ; m. David S. Messinger.

Timothy T., b. Jan. 7, 1817 ; m. Mary Stockman.

Lydia A., b. May 4, 1821 ; d. Sept. 2, 1823.

Frances A., b. July 3, 1826 ; m. Abram P. Paichard.

Sarah M., b. May 2, 1839.

William Sawyer, my brother, was a man of much prominence in Charlestown. He was a graduate of Harvard College in the class of 1828. A lawyer by profession ; member of the Legislature ; Chairman of the Board of Selectmen, and of the School Committee, etc., etc. He was killed while crossing the Fitchburg Railroad in his carriage with his family. His eldest daughter was also killed. The accident happened at Waltham, where he had a short time before erected, and moved into, an elegant residence.

Oliver Sawyer's father died when he was young, and, August 5, 1740, his mother was appointed his guardian. The births of his children are on the Haverhill records. .

William Sawyer married Hannah Snow. He next married Widow Hannah Snow, whose maiden name was Brickett, Oct. 27, 1791. He last married Widow Bethiah W. Wyman, Sept 17, 1807.

The *first* Joshua Sawyer is on the tax list of Woburn as early as the year 1670. He is supposed to be the son of Thomas and Mary Sawyer of Lancaster. His children were all born in Woburn. His son, the *second* Joshua, married Mary Carter of Woburn, May 22, 1706. His widow's name appears on the tax list after his death. Wyman says in his book : " Joshua Sawyer *of Lancaster*, who married Mary Carter, daughter of Thomas, son of Rev. Thomas of Woburn, was taxed for an estate in Charlestown in 1734."

The following letter was received from D. W. MANCHESTER of Cleveland, Ohio. It relates to the descendants of WILLIAM SAWYER of Newbury, who was the brother of THOMAS SAWYER of Lancaster. The letter must speak for itself to the friends to whom it relates:

CLEVELAND, O., May 3, 1882.

AMORY CARTER, ESQ., WORCESTER, MASS.:

Dear Sir:—The following record of a Sawyer family I copied, in 1876, from the original sheet manuscript record, then in possession of Mr. Pardon Williston of Tiverton, R. I.; a man who was then nearly 90 years of age, and who has since died. The record had been in his family many years. You may be able to trace this branch, and it may be of some use to you:

Josiah Sawyer, Sen., born Jan. 20, 1681; married, Dec. 20, 1705, Martha Seabury of Duxbury, Mass. Josiah was son of William of Newbury, born 1656, and was son of William who was in Salem in 1643. Children:

John, b. Feb. 2, 1707; single; d. May, 1793.
Hannah, b. Nov. 17, 1709; m. J. W.; d. 1780.
Mirey, b. Jan. 28, 1712; m. S. R.
Mary, b. Aug. 28, 1714; m. G. B.; d. March 4, 1775.
Abigail, b. Oct. 4, 1716; m. J. T.; d. 1777.
Josiah, b. May 15, 1722; m. S. P.; d. Sept. 18, 1792.
Russialla, b. 1724; d. 1752.

Hannah, born 1709; married Aug. 27, 1730, John Williston, born 1705, son of John, born 1650; wife Abigail had daughter Anna, born 1683, who married Edward Manchester; William M. married Mary Irish, daughter of John I. (2) and Thankful Wilbur; John Irish (1) married Deborah Church, sister of Col. Benj. Church, of Indian wars fame; Benj. C. married Alice Southworth, grand-daughter of Gov. Bradford. Benj. C., as you will perhaps remember, cut off the head of King Phillip with a sword, which, as I now recollect it, was made at a blacksmith's shop in Little Compton, R. I., where Mrs. Irish lived. The immediate cause of the death of Col. Benjamin was being thrown from his horse on to a large stone while visiting his sister, Mrs. Irish at Little Compton. Benjamin was born at Duxbury, Mass., in 1639; was son of Joseph, born 1613. I do not know for whom any of the initials stand in the Sawyer record except those of John Williston who married Hannah S. Very truly, etc.,

D. W MANCHESTER.

HAVERHILL SAWYERS.

The following sketch is from the pen of Mrs. J. E. Taft.
Probably relates to a branch of the Sawyer family who descended
from Samuel, the son of Wm. Sawyer of Newbury, whose de-
scendants were quite numerous in and around Haverhill. The
Jonathan and Nathaniel named by her, who married sisters and
settled in Westminster, Mass., were probably descendants from
Samuel Sawyer. Mrs. Taft was the sister of the late Judge
Aaron Sawyer, of Nashua, N. H. He was a man of much note
and influence in Hillsboro' County, as was evident from an ex-
tended obituary notice, published at the time of his decease.
The obituary was too extensive to be included in this work.
Enough to say that it was very complimentary, and no doubt
well deserving. He was cousin to Judge Geo. Y. Sawyer, also
of Nashua, with whom the editor had some correspondence, but
he died suddenly without any sketch of his life, except that he
was born in Westminster, Mass., and his father's name was William: no doubt the William mentioned in the following genealogical sketch :

W. L. SAWYER, 42 Wilmot St., PORTLAND, Me.

Two brothers, Jonathan and Nathaniel Sawyer, married
sisters by the name of Flint, from Reading, and settled in Westminster Jonathan was my grandfather. William Sawyer of
Reading, Mass., went to Bradford, N. H.,—a descendant of
William of 1643. Thomas Sawyer settled in Worcester, Mass.
Ex-Senator Sawyer descended from him. His name, Frederic H.
I have heard of Prof. Sawyer, of Boston. a Universalist minister
and an aged man ; also an Amos Sawyer. of Northampton, Mass.,
who is one of seventeen children. He has a pocket-book in his
possession which has been handed down five generations.

Mrs. Hannah Graves. of Monson. Mass., says she never
knew of a Sawyer having committed a State prison or jail offence.

My grandfather lived in Westminster, Mass. Married Miss Jerusha Flint. The children were Eli, Nathaniel, Amos, William, Aaron Flint,—the last my father's name. The daughters were Rachel and Caroline. Rachel married a Mr. Edgell, and lived in Westminster. Caroline married a Mr. Brooks and lived in Rutland, Vt. Nathaniel lived in Rutland, Vt., and was deacon of the Methodist Church. Eli and Amos lived in Westminster. William was a graduate of Harvard College, studied law in Portsmouth, and married Miss Mary Eaton of that place, and practiced in Wakefield, N. H. Aaron Flint, a graduate of Dartmouth College, studied law at Amherst, N. H., with the Hon. C. H. Atherton, father of Senator C. G. Atherton ; practiced at the Hillsboro' bar,—both at Mt. Vernon and Nashua. He was a gentleman of the old school, dignified, courteous and affable. After his death, which occurred suddenly of heart disease, his clients knew not where to go, they had such confidence in him. He married Hannah Locke, of Fitchburg. Five of his six children lived to mature age. Their names were Samuel Locke, Charlotte Locke, Aaron Worcester, Flint Holyoke and Catherine Adams.

Samuel's children that lived to mature age are Mary Greene, Aaron Flint, Thomas Calloway and Fanny Ingalls. Samuel married Mary Calloway and resides in Independence, Mo.; has held the office of Judge and Representative to Congress.

Charlotte married Aaron P. Hughes, who studied law with Aaron F. Sawyer, and practiced law in Nashua until his death. Her sons are James A. Dupee and Aaron Porter, both graduates of Dartmouth College. You will learn of Aaron in the obituary notice. Catherine Adams married John E. Taft, and resides in Worcester, Mass. Has two children : Charles Whiting and Aaron Sawyer.

Perhaps I had better say that Aaron W. had two wives. The first, Fanny Ingalls of N. Y.; the second Fanny Winch of Nashua. His children living are Fanny Locke and William.

Flint married Martha Coburn, who still lives in Nashua. He died some years since.

MRS. J. E. TAFT.

MORE ABOUT THE NEWBURY SAWYERS.

James the son of William, of Newbury, settled in Gloucester, and had a numerous family of children by first and second wife. Savage says of the third generation of Sawyers that they are too numerous to mention. The Gloucester Sawyers are too numerous for me to mention, as I cannot read Babson's history of Gloucester, but will refer my readers to that history for further information. Probably Samuel E. Sawyer, Esq., now of Gloucester, is a descendant of James of Newbury, and I refer to him as well as Babson's History. J. Brown Lord, Esq., whose communication is to be seen in the preceding pages claims that his great-great-grandfather was Francis Sawyer of Ipswich. That Francis was probably the grandson of William of Newbury, who had two sons by the name of Francis, one by the first wife who died in childhood, another by the second wife who lived to adult age, probably that second Francis was the father of Francis of Ipswich. That I have not given a more extensive account of the Newbury Sawyers, I must plead blindness for my excuse, and trust in their charity.

The following communication is from Miss ELLEN M. SAWYER, daughter of the late Dr. SAMUEL SAWYER of Cambridge, which includes the genealogy and the list of graduates from Harvard College, taken from the manuscript of Dr. SAWYER:

DESCENDANTS OF ELISHA SAWYER.

Elisha, son of Elisha, lived in Sterling. He held a lieutenant's commission in the army under Washington, and was with him at White Plains and Valley Forge. He married Patience Bennett of Boylston, Oct. 31, 1765; afterwards Widow Mary Belknap, daughter of Zachariah and Mary (Gardner)

Flagg, of Woburn, May 3, 1770 ; after her death (about
1781) he married the widow Mary Bowker, of Sterling, Oct.
14, 1802. Children by first wife :

Paul, b. Oct. 20, 1767 ; m. Hannah Mudge, of Lynn. He
lived many years in Plymouth, Vt., but finally removed
to Royalton, N. Y., where he died, April 28, 1845. After
the death of his wife, Hannah, he married successively
two other wives, but left no children by either.

Children by second wife :

William, b. April 13, 1772; settled in Sterling and died
March 28, 1827.

Samuel Flagg, b. Feb. 20, 1774 ; settled in Cambridge.

John b. Aug. 11, 1776 ; d. aged 12.

Franklin, b. Jan. 15, 1778 ; settled in Cambridge.

Elisha, b. about 1780 ; d. at age of 4.

Children by third wife : Jason, Charles, and Lois.

William married Nancy Carter, Jan. 1, 1800 ; she was born July
28, 1777; died July 21, 1844; he died March 28, 1827.
Children as follows :

Eliza, b. May 26, 1801 ; m. George P. Smith of Liverpool,
N. S., who settled in Boston.

Mary, b. March 27, 1803 ; m., 1st, Abram Haley, April 27,
1834, by whom she had one daughter, Louisa, who married
the Rev. W. P. Tilden of Boston; after the death of Mr.
Haley, in Nov. 16, 1846, she married John D. Pratt of
Fitchburg, Nov. 1854.

Nancy, born Jan. 12, 1806 ; married Hiram Davis, of Shir-
ley, Jan., 1828; settled in Fitchburg. Children as follows :

William Sawyer, b. Jan. 6, 1829 ; d. April 3, 1837.

Helen Maria, b. Dec. 17, 1831.

Frederick H., b. Nov. 18, 1833.

William Sawyer, b. Jan. 27, 1838 ; d. young.

Isabella A., b. Sept. 22, 1839.

Harriet Elizabeth, b. March 17, 1843 ; d. Oct. 21, 1843.

Franklin, b. July 1, 1808 ; d. May 21, 1812.

Susan, born Feb. 7, 1813 : married Isaac Pulsifer, of Gloucester, Sept. 2, 1838 ; removed to Cambridge, July, 1855.
Children as follows :

George Franklin, b. June 12, 1839.

Susan, b. Dec. 20, 1842 ; d. Nov. 1845.

Charles, b. June 17, 1848 ; d. July, 1849.

Charles Henry, b. May 25, 1850.

William Franklin, born Dec. 6 or 7, 1814, married Nancy
Ordway, April, 1841 ; settled in Sterling.

Caroline Augusta, b. Aug 2, 1819.

Samuel Flagg, married Patience Learned, of Watertown, Mass.,
Feb. 16, 1800 ; she was born Aug. 30, 1778 ; died 1863 ;
he died April 16, 1853. Children as follows :

Samuel, b. March 20, 1804 ; d. Jan. 4, 1859.

Mary Ann, born Jan. 15, 1806 ; married Dr. Jeremiah H.
Brower, March 26, 1835 ; he was born in New York City,
June 30, 1799 ; settled in Lawrenceburg, Ind. Children
as follows :

Elizabeth Hannah, b. Feb. 6, 1836 ; d. Sept. 26, 1840.

Martha Sawyer, b. Sept. 10, 1837.

Samuel Sawyer, b. July 1, 1844 ; d. April, 1872.

Susan Dunn, b. Sept. 15, 1847 ; d. 1849.

Louisa, born April 7, 1808 ; married William Bradford
Thurston, of Newport, R. I.; died in Indianapolis, Ind.,
Jan. 12, 1874. Children as follows :

Moses, b. Oct. 18, 1837 ; d. Feb. 20, 1838.

Caroline Louisa, b. Oct. 1, 1838.

Charles Prindle, b. May, 1843.

William Bradford, b. May, 1848.

Martha, born Feb. 14, 1810 ; married Rev. Hubbard Lawrence, Sept. 28, 1841 ; he was born at St. Johnsbury, Vt.,
May 1, 1811 ; settled in Ohio. Children as follows :

Martha Elizabeth, b. Sept. 11, 1842.

Mary Clarissa, b. Sept. 22, 1844 ; d. Feb. 14, 1851.

Hubbard, b. May 20, 1846; d. Nov., 1881; m. Alice Lawrence, Oct. 30, 1867.

John James, b. May 29, 1848; m. Ella Goss.

Mary Clarissa, b. July 29, 1852; d. Sept. 11, 1853.

Caroline., b. May 12, 1812; d. Sept. 23, 1818.

John James, b. July 29, 1814; m., 1st, Anna Maria, daughter of Isaac and Lucy (Green) Tufts, Oct. 6, 1850; d. Sept. 5, 1871; 2d, Louisa Tufts, m. Dec. 16, 1873. Served in the navy during the Mexican War; lives in Somerville, Mass.; is assistant Clerk of the Courts of Middlesex Co.

Lucy Downing, b. Sept. 29, 1816; d. Oct. 4, 1872; lives at Indianapolis, Ind.

Franklin Sawyer died in Kansas aged 91; married Mary Hastings, of Cambridge, Feb. 20, 1806; she was born Oct. 1, 1786; died May 31, 1853. Children as follows:

Elizabeth, b. Sept. 30, 1807; m. Hannibel Wright, Oct. 15, 1830; he was born in Templeton, Feb. 11, 1805; d. in Detroit, Mich., Sept. 3, 1834; she d. in Cambridge, Mass., Dec. 18, 1844; left children as follows:

Franklin Sawyer, b. Aug. 26, 1831; d. at Ironton, Ohio.

Charles Learned, b. Aug. 14, 1834; settled in Alton, Ill.

Franklin, b. June 18, 1809.

Evelina, b. Sept. 9. 1811; d. Feb. 22, 1838.

Ann Lucretia, b. Sept. 5, 1814; d. May 21, 1840.

Eliza Jane, b. April 18, 1817; d. ——.

Caroline Amelia Augusta, b. May 19, 1819; m. Charles Ingersoll, of Boston, July 31, 1846. Children as follows:

William M., b. June 8, 1847.

Mary Elizabeth, b. Sept. 5, 1848; d. Oct. 13, 1849, at Newport, Ohio.

Caroline Amelia, twin, b. Sept. 21, 1850; d. Feb. 22, 1854.

Charles Edward, twin, b. Sept. 21, 1850; d. Sept. 12, 1851.

Eliza, b. Sept. 6, 1852; d. ——.

Jane Lucretia, b. Aug. 22, 1854; d. ——.

Emily Caroline, b. June 6, 1856; d. ——.

William Franklin married Nancy Ordway, April, 1841. Had one child: Charles S., b. June 24, 1858; d. Aug. 7, 1858.

*Samuel married Lucy Tufts, daughter of Isaac and Lucy (Green) Tufts, of Charlestown, Nov. 21, 1833. Children as follows:

Mary Ann Brower, b. March 8, 1835.

Lucy Tufts, b. Oct. 5, 1836.

Caroline Louisa, b. Sept. 7, 1838.

Ellen Maria, b. April 16, 1840.

Martha Elizabeth, b. June 18, 1842.

Evelyn Augusta, b. May 11, 1844.

†Franklin married Sarah Martha Loring, daughter of Braddock and Sarah (Shattuck) Loring, of New Orleans, June 1, 1834; she was born Dec. 9, 1813; d. Jan. 4, 1867. Children as follows:

Sarah Elizabeth, b. Jan. 23, 1835; lived two days.

Emily Caroline, b. Feb. 19, 1836; d. about 1862 in New Orleans.

Loring, b. Nov. 2, 1837; an officer in the Confederate Army; killed in second battle of Manassas.

Frank, b. June 15, 1839; d. Oct. 31, 1840.

Frank Hastings, b. April 14, 1841; served in Confederate Army; d. ——.

John Talbott, b. Feb. 4, 1843; m. Elizabeth McKnight, of New Orleans; clergyman.

Sarah Pitts, b. Jan. 30, 1844; m. Charles McKnight, of New Orleans, La.

Howard, b. ——; d. in New Orleans, ——.

---

*He graduated at Harvard College in 1826, and at Harvard Medical School 831; settled as physician and surgeon in Fairhaven, Mass., in 1833. In 1849 ent to San Francisco, Cal., and was one of the founders of the first medi- ociety in San Francisco; in April, 1853, he returned to Cambridge, where 1 Jan. 4, 1859.

ranklin graduated at Harvard College in 1830, where he also studied went to Detroit, Michigan, in 1831; was Superintendent of Public In- in that State in 1841 and '42; he then went to New Orleans, where he rintendent of Public Instruction two years. In 1845 he took the edi- the *New Orleans Daily Tropic*; in 1847, his health failing, he was emove again to the North, and he finally established himself in Cam- native place, where he entered into the practice of his profession, one of the editors of *The Christian Watchman*; was a member of e City Council, and a Representative in the State Legislature at death, which occurred on Nov. 18, 1851.

GRADUATES OF HARVARD COLLEGE.

Micajah, 1756, Mr., M. D. 1793, A. A. et M. M. S. S.; became an eminent physician; he was one of the earliest members of the M. M. S. S., having joined at its first formation in 1781; he died Sept. 29, 1815, aged 78.

Amos, 1765, Mr.; d. 1769; age, 25; was pastor elect of the First Church in Danvers, but died probably before ordination, Sept. 21, 1769. The following is from his tombstone in North Reading.

"IN MEMORY OF AMOS SAWYER, A. M.,
Elect Pastor of the First Church of Christ in Danvers,
Who departed this life,
September 21, 1769, in his 26th year.

When Clark the great was called to the superior skies,
To fill the gap his flock on Sawyer set their eyes;
In work divine his help they crave; his help was given,
But God withheld the gift,—the Giver took to Heaven."

Ebenezer, 1768, (spelled Sayer on catalogue), Mr.; d. 1778.
William, 1788, Mr.; M. B., 1792; M. D., 1811; d. 1859.

Artemas, 1793; distinguished scholar; was Professor in the University of Ohio, at Athens; he was from Lancaster, Mass.; d. 1815.

William, 1800; b. at Westminster, Oct. 26, 1775; lawyer; settled in Wakefield, N. H.; d. 1860.

Samuel, 1826, Mr.: M. D., 1831; M. M. S. S.; d. 1859.
William, 1828; b. Dec. 15, 1807; d. May 24, 1852.
Franklin, 1830; lawyer; d. 1851.
Frederic Adolphus, 1844, U. S. Senator.
Albert Franklin, 1849; M. D. 1852.

Thomas Jefferson, Middlebury College, 1829, et Mr., Middlebury, 1833 ; S. T. D. in College Tufts Theol. Christ. Prof.; S. T. D., Harvard College, 1850 ; elected President of Tufts' College, Medford, Mass., 1852.

George Carleton, 1855.

Frederick Augustus, M. D. 1856., M. M. S. S.

Amory Pollard, 1858; d. 1860.

John Woodbury, M. D. 1859, M. M. S. S.

Wesley Caleb, 1861, Mr. Ph. D. Gott. 1870.

Benjamin Addison, M. D. 1865, M. M. S. S.

Edward, M. D. 1865, M. M. S. S.

Francis Haller, 1872.

Edward Warren, M. D. 1873, M. M. S. S.

Robert William, 1874.

George Augustus, 1877.

William Brewster, M. D. 1879 ; Amherst, 1875.

HARVARD SAWYERS.

Hon. Philetus Sawyer was a descendant from the Harvard branch of Sawyers.

Caleb Sawyer, the fifth son of Thomas Sawyer of Lancaster, was born in 1659; married Sarah Houghton, and settled in that part of Lancaster which was afterwards set off in Harvard. He became the first progenitor of what is known as the Harvard branch of Sawyers. He had among others a son whose name was Jonathan. He (Jonathan) had two sons by the name of Caleb and Seth. Caleb settled in Westmoreland, N. H., and had four sons, whose names were Caleb, Ephraim, Jonathan and Menassah. Caleb settled on the home place; Ephraim settled as a Baptist minister in Whiting, Vt.; Jonathan was killed at the building of Fort Ticonderoga, and Menassah served as surgeon in the Revolutionary Army, as is shown by the letter of Hon. W. H. Sawyer. It was with great difficulty that the parentage of Caleb of Westmoreland was ascertained. After two full years of diligent search it came through Miss Ellen M. Sawyer, daughter of the late Dr. Samuel Sawyer of Cambridge, to whom was assigned the duty of bringing out a genealogy of the Sawyers, but did not live to succeed. From his papers Miss Ellen M. Sawyer discovered that Caleb, of Westmoreland, was the son of Jonathan of Harvard, Mass., and grandson of Caleb first, and thus the connection between the Vermont and New York Sawyers, with Thomas, Sen., of Lancaster, who was the son of John Sawyer, a farmer of Lincolnshire, England.   )

It may not be improper here to show that Hon. Philetus Sawyer, who holds the highest office under the United States Government, except the Presidency, Hon. W. H. Sawyer, who has been Judge of the Supreme Court of New York, Hon. Lorenzo Sawyer, of San Francisco, and many other Sawyers, who have held high places under the United States Government, and the highest places in our institutions of learning, are descended from the laboring classes of England, who had no possible chance of obtaining an education under her system of laws. Copies of Wills and Deeds will be herein exhibited which were signed by Thomas Sawyer, Sen., and Thomas, Jr., by "making their mark." Neither of them could read or write, and yet they were the most prominent men in building up the old town of Lancaster. The Colonial records show that Thomas Sawyer represented the town in the Legislature, and received several appointments from the Government in the arrangement of business affairs of the town. From that family has arisen a class of men in this country which are second to none other. They have no aristocratic title to fall back upon, and they ask for no "coat-of-arms" to exhibit, and refer to no honorary pedigree. They have risen by their own merits and the merits of the institutions under which they lived. They stand square on their feet and need no leaning post. They are independent of all others, so far as honor is concerned.

Seth Sawyer, brother of Caleb second, had two sons whose names were Jonathan and Caleb. Jonathan had a son Luke, who had a son Jonathan, who was the father of Wilbur Fiske Sawyer, now living on the home estate in Harvard ; also, Wesley C. Sawyer, who is Professor in Lawrence University in Wisconsin.

Caleb third, brother of Jonathan second, had a son by the name of Phineas, who built the first cotton factory in Massachusetts. It was situated in Marlborough upon the Assabet River. It was built in 1806. The Lowell factories were built in 1812. The Peace of 1815 let in the English cottons, and Sawyer had to stop his mill. I knew the mill well for many years, and it stood idle a long while. It was burned down and never reappeared. There was a saw and grist mill on the same premises, and while cutting out a frozen water-wheel it started suddenly and he fell and was killed. A sketch of his family is here appended. It was written by Dr. Spaulding of New Hampshire, and was furnished the editor by Col. Charles H. Sawyer, of the Sawyer Woolen Mills Co., in Dover, N. H.:

Phineas Sawyer was born at Harvard, Mass., in 1768. He went to Marlborough, Mass., now Hudson, in 1800. He bought a mill property there, consisting of a saw, grist, and wire-drawing mill. In 1806 he built a cotton mill, and operated it until the close of the war in 1815. It required in those days immense enterprise and energy to project and carry on such a work as a cotton factory. The machinery was procured from Rhode Island. The ginning machine had not yet come into general use. The cotton, when received, was distributed among the farmers to have the seeds picked out one by one by their families. It was carded and spun by water power at the mill. It was then sent out again among the farmers to be woven into cloth. Phineas Sawyer was a man of great independence of character, self-reliant, and full of courage. These qualities, so conspicuous in his business affairs, shone out with undiminished power in his religious life. He lived at a time in Massachusetts when Methodism was regarded with special disfavor. But Mr. Sawyer, believing that the Methodists were right, believing so with all his heart, and the petty persecutions to which his faith was subjected, only intensified his zeal and loyalty. His house was the home for all traveling Methodists, and the place where they gathered for religious worship. He was well versed in the best Methodist literature of his time. He stands forth in the annals of his church as one of the foremost men for sagacity, boldness, and piety, in the Needham circuit He had for his wife a worthy helpmeet, Hannah Whitney, of Harvard. She was as ardently attached to Methodism as was her husband, and bore her full share of service and sacrifice for it in its days of weakness and persecution. The sudden death of her husband, which took place in 1820, left Mrs. Sawyer to provide for the support of twelve children, the youngest, Jonathan, being then two years old. This truly noble woman, with but little means, faced the difficulties before her with an unflinching spirit of faith and hopefulness. It required superlative fortitude, finest sagacity, and sternest self-sacrifice to have enabled this mother to successfully rear these twelve children, give to them a good education, and establish all of them in respectable positions in the world. She continued to live in Marlborough some nine years, leasing the property. In 1829 she went to Lowell, where she lived twenty years, dying there in 1849, greatly respected by all who knew her, and held in honor and affection by her many children.

Jonathan Sawyer, the subject of this sketch, was the youngest child of Phineas. He was born at Marlborough, Mass., in 1817. He went with his mother and other members of the family when he was twelve years old to Lowell, where, for the next few years, he attended school. He was a member of the first class that entered the high school of that city, having among his mates Hon. Benjamin F. Butler, Gov. E. A. Straw, and G. V. Fox, Assistant Secretary of the Navy. Bishop Thomas M. Clark was the teacher of this school. On account of a severe sickness, young Sawyer, at sixteen years of age, left school, and while re- cruiting his health made a visit to his brother, Alfred Ira Sawyer, who, after some experience as a dyer at Amesbury and Great Falls, had come, in 1824, to Dover, N. H., where he was operating a grist mill, a custom carding and a cloth-dressing mill, converting the last into a flannel mill. Jonathan remained in Dover two years, going to school and working for his brother. In the fall of 1835 he returned to Lowell. His mother, for the purpose of conferring upon her son a complete education, sent him to the great Methodist school at Wilbraham, which at that time was a most flourishing preparatory school for the Wesleyan University at Middleton, Conn. Here he remained two terms, when at nineteen years of age he returned to Lowell, he went into a woolen establishment as a dyer. Afterwards he went into this business on his own account, and continued in it until 1839. During the latter part of this time he was not so engrossed in his business but that he found time to make frequent visits to New Ipswich, where Miss Martha Perkins, of Barnard, Vt., was attending school. In 1839 they were married, and went to Watertown, N. Y., where Mr. Sawyer became the Superintendent of the Hamilton Woolen Company. After two and a half years, Mr. Sawyer went into business for the manufacture of satinets. In 1850, his brother Alfred having died at Dover, N. H., the year before, and the children being too young to carry on the business, Mr. Jonathan Sawyer assumed its control in connection with his brother Zenas. Two years later Zenas retired, and Francis A. Sawyer, who had been a prominent builder in Boston, became a partner with Jonathan, the object being to continue the manufacture of woolen flannels. In 1858 the property below, known as the " Moses Mill," another flannel manufactory, was purchased. This mill was enlarged in 1860 to four sets of machinery, and again in 1863 to eight, and in 1880 and 1882 to sixteen sets. The old machinery is now completely replaced by new. The old mill that was started in 1832 was, in 1872, replaced by the present substantial structure, which contains fourteen sets of machinery, with preparing and finishing machinery for the thirty sets in both mills. Since 1866 the attention of these noted manufacturers has been entirely devoted to the manufacture of fine fancy cassimere cloths and suitings. Already they have established for these goods a foremost place in their class. At the Centennial Exhibition, at Philadelphia, a medal and diploma were awarded the Sawyer goods, for their " high intrinsic merit." The business has, since 1873, been carried on as a corporation, having a capitol of six hundred thousand dollars. The corporation consists of the old firm of F. A. and J. Sawyer, and Charles H. Sawyer, the present agent of the establishment. In 1866 this company made a bold innovation on the method that was so long in vogue among manufacturers, of consigning their goods to Commission Houses. The undertaking upon which this company entered, of selling their own goods, was met with great opposition ; but their boldness and foresight have already been justified by the success which they have made, and the adoption of their methods by other manufacturers. This establishment can now look back upon a half-century of remarkable history. The unmarred reputation for strictest integrity which these managers have won, their far-reaching enterprise, and the unsurpassed excellence of their fabrics, have enabled them to prosperously pass through all the financial depressions and panics which so many times have swept over the country during this long period.

Mr. Jonathan Sawyer, with his vigor of mind and body still unimpaired, lives in his elegant mansion, which looks out upon a magnificent picture of woods, and vale, and mountain range, and down upon the busy scene of his many years of tireless industry. He loves his home, in the adornment of which his fine taste finds full play. When free from business he is always there. He loves his books, and his conversation shows an unusual breadth of reading in science, history, and politics. He is possessed of

14

a strong, clear intellect, a calm dispassionate judgment and sympathies which always bring him to the side of the wronged and the suffering. At a time when anti-slavery sentiments were unpopular, Mr. Sawyer was free in their utterance, and was among the first to form the Free-soil party. Since the organization of the Republican party, Mr. Sawyer has been among its strongest supporters. He has persistently declined the many offices of honor and profit which those acquainted with his large intelligence, and sagacity, and stainless honesty have sought to confer upon him. He is abundantly content to exercise his business powers in developing still more the great manufactory, and his affections upon his household and his chosen friends, and his public spirit in helping every worthy cause and person in the community. The children of Mr. Sawyer, all of whom have grown up to maturity, are Charles Henry, Mary Elizabeth, Francis Asbury, Roswell Douglas, Martha Frances, Alice May, and Frederick Jonathan.

LETTER FROM HON. PHILETUS SAWYER;
United States Senator from Oshkosh, Wisconsin.

My grandfather was Ephraim Sawyer, a Baptist preacher in Vermont and New Hampshire. My father's name was Ephraim Sawyer; he also lived in Vermont; removed from there into Essex County, State of New York, in 1817, when I was about a year old. He had five sons:—Chauncy P. Sawyer, farmer and blacksmith, now lives in Ticonderoga, Essex County, N. Y. He has two sons, Chauncy and John, are living with him. Another son is Ephraim P. Sawyer, farmer, lives at Burlington, Racine County, Wis. He has three sons now living. I am the next son, Philetus Sawyer. I have one son, Edgar P. Sawyer, living at Oshkosh, who is in the lumber business in connection with myself, under the firm name of P. Sawyer & Son. I have a grandson Philetus Edgar Sawyer, about 8 years old. My next brother is Professor Alonzo J. Sawyer, living in Chicago, Illinois; has been a Professor in the Douglas University, Chicago, for many years. He has also two sons. The youngest brother is Andrew Sawyer. He is a blacksmith and carriage and plow manufacturer at Burlington, Racine County, Wis., and has two sons. My brothers are all well provided with this world's goods.　　　　　PHILETUS SAWYER.

Since the above letter was written, Philetus Sawyer has been elected United States Senator from Wisconsin, and the following sketch of his life is taken from a Western newspaper, about the the time of his election:

SENATOR SAWYER, OF WISCONSIN.

" Hon. Philetus Sawyer, the new Senator-elect from Wisconsin, though he has been voluntarily out of public life since 1875, is not an untried or inexperienced man in the National Legislature, and will enter the Senate with a reputation established as an energetic and sagacious legislator.

Mr. Sawyer was born in Vermont, September 22, 1816, and is therefore now sixty-four years of age. He was not born great, or wealthy, for his father was a farmer and blacksmith at a time when and in a region where those employments promised but little but hard work and a subsistence. He has not had greatness thrust upon him by adventitious circumstances, for there has been nothing accidental in the career which has now reached a place in the highest representative body in the world. Whatever of wealth and of honor in station and reputation he has attained, has been achieved by an honest and industrious use of the faculties with which nature endowed him, and of the opportunities which were open to all competitors.

When he was a year old his father removed to Essex County, N. Y., where his childhood and youth were passed among the mountains and forests of the Adirondacks. His early life, like that of most of the dwellers in that region, was one of manual labor, with only such opportunities for education as the common schools of that time and place furnished for the children of those whose life work was to toil for bread and raiment.

There is something almost pathetic in the contemplation of such a beginning to a career every way so successful as Mr. Sawyer's. He had not that instinctive craving for the learning of the schools, which from a very humble beginning, has made of the

President-elect one of the most scholarly statesmen of his time. But in every step and in every phase of his life, Mr. Sawyer has been constantly acquiring that knowledge of men and affairs, which is a condition of leadership and success in a generation eminently practical and looking mainly to material results.

At seventeen, by an arrangement with his father, Mr. Sawyer became the master of his own time and labor. These he employed so successfully that in 1847, at the age of thirty-one, he was enabled to seek a more profitable field for his future efforts in Wisconsin, with a capital of about two thousand dollars. Two seasons of not very successful farming in his new home, turned his thoughts to his former occupation of " logging " and lumbering. The great Wolf River pinery was then scarcely touched. To the practical lumbermen it offered a prospect for accumulating wealth, and in December, 1849, Mr. Sawyer removed to the village of Algoma, now in the city of Oshkosh. Here, the following season, he took a contract to run, and subsequently rented, and finally purchased a saw mill which had nearly ruined its owners, and from that to the present time his career as a business man has been a constant success. Where others have failed he has succeeded. When others have stood still he has advanced. His industry and sagacity have been so rewarded that his financial standing is now in the front rank among the solid men of Wisconsin.

His reputation for integrity, open-handed generosity in his dealings, and for sound judgment in business enterprises, has been uniform and doubtless has contributed to his success.

It is inevitable that such a man should be called into the public service in a new and thriving country.

Mr. Sawyer served several years in the Common Council of the young city of his residence. In 1857 and in 1861, he was a member of the State Legislature. He served as Mayor two years. In 1864 he was clothed with full power and discretion to compromise and settle the bonded debt of the city, which he accomplished on exceedingly favorable terms. In 1862, though strongly solicited, he declined on account of his private business, to become a candidate for Congress. He was a Republican of free soil democratic antecedents. In 1862 the district elected a Democratic candidate by a majority of over one thousand. Two years later, Mr. Sawyer consented to be a candidate and was elected by a majority of about three thousand. From 1865 to 1875 he was continued in the House of Representatives and retired, after a continuous service of ten years, only because he refused to be a candidate for re-election.

His record as a member of Congress is part of the history of that time. He was one term chairman of the Committee on Government Expenditures. In the 43d Congress he was chairman of the Pacific R. R. Committee. Eight years he was on the Committee on Commerce. Six years he was second member on that committee and during a large portion of that time the acting chairman. Therefore, it became his duty several times, to report and take charge of the bills making appropriations for rivers and harbors, and a fair illustration of the confidence of his fellow members is found in the fact that such bills appropriating millions were sometimes passed under suspension of the rules when reported and vouched for by him.

Mr. Sawyer is not fitted by nature, training or inclination for speech making in Congress. But his acknowledged influence and sound judgment on matters of practical legislation have been of more influence in obtaining and retaining the confidence of the people of Wisconsin, than would any number of speeches reported in the *Congressional Record*, and if the future may be judged by the past, he will be a useful and influential senator. In any legislative body, a clear headed man of affairs, who does not form conclusions from superficial examinations and brings strict integrity, as well as sound judgment to the work of legislation, is a valuable and a respected member. Such a member Mr. Sawyer has always been heretofore and doubtless will be in his new position "

110

LETTER FROM HON. W. H. SAWYER.

CANTON, N. Y., JUNE 9, 1881.

My great-grandfather's name was Caleb, and he resided, during the early years of my grandfather's life, about 15 miles from Boston, I think in Walpole. He afterwards removed with his family to Westmoreland, in New Hampshire. He had four sons, viz: Caleb, Jonathan, Ephraim and Menassah. Caleb held the homestead at Westmoreland. Jonathan was killed at Ticonderoga, in the State of New York, at the time of building that fort. Ephraim became a Baptist clergymen. Menassah, who was my grandfather, died at Potsdam, in this State, in March, 1842. He was a seargent in the Union Army of the Revolution; was connected with Putnam's Rangers; was in the battle of Bennington under Starke, and at the battle of Stony Point under Gen. Wayne. He married Bulah Howe of Sudbury, Mass.; had four sons: Menassah, Martin, Willard and George. Menassah had two sons, John and George. John is living in Fulton, Oswego County, N. Y. George died last year at Syracuse, N. Y., leaving two sons. Azariah H. Sawyer, who lives at Watertown, N. Y., and has been County Judge of that (Jefferson) County. George still lives at Syracuse, N. Y. Willard had two sons, Charles and James. Charles lives in Illinois somewhere, and James died a few years ago at Fort Covington, this State, leaving daughters but no sons. Martin had no sons. George Rex, my father, was born in Westmoreland, N. H., in 1787, and died at Potsdam, N. Y., in 1855. He left one son, W. H. Sawyer, and six daughter. W. H. Sawyer, born Oct. 15, 1826; married Marion Clark, Sept., 1854, and has seven sons and two daughters, viz: George C., Lawrence C., Darius C., William T., Guy B., Benjamin M. and Hugh A. Daughters: Marion and Mary. W. H. Sawyer is a lawyer, and has been Judge of the Supreme Court of this State. You will see he has guarded so far as may be against the line running out with him. Neither George of Syracuse, nor A. H. of Watertown have any sons, though both have daughters. From this brief synopsis you may be able to place properly my branch of this extensive family. Yours very truly,

W. H. SAWYER.

WESLEY CALEB SAWYER.

The following sketch is taken from a Wisconsin newspaper :

" Prof. Wesley Caleb Sawyer, of Lawrence University, was born in Harvard, Mass., Aug. 26, 1839, on the homestead of the Sawyer family for six generations. He was prepared for college at Wilbraham Academy, under Dr. Miner Raymond. Went through Harvard College in the class of 1861, taking prizes in both writing and speaking. Soon after his graduation, he enlisted as a private soldier under Henry Wilson, who was organizing a regiment in Massachusetts, and was promoted to the captaincy before leaving the State. He passed unharmed through the naval and land battles of Roanoke Island, and went with Gen. Burnside up the Neuse River. In the battle of Newberne he was hit by a rebel cannon ball, carrying away his left leg. He, however, recovered the ball and now uses it as a match safe, it being a case shot. As soon as able, he engaged in the canvass of his own State to encourage enlistments by holding public meetings. He was then offered the command of an artillery regiment, which he declined because unacquainted with that branch of the service. He was then appointed commandant of " Camp Stevens," at Groton, Mass., and there organized and trained the Fifty-third Massachusetts infantry. He afterwards passed a full course of study in the Methodist Theological School at Concord, N. H., joined the New England Conference of the M. E. Church, and preached one year at Maplewood, near Boston. Then asked leave of absence to travel in Europe. Visited England, Ireland, Scotland, Germany, Russia, Poland, Switzerland, France and Denmark. Studied three years in Germany and one in France, being on the German side of the line during the Franco-German war ; attended lectures in Berlin University, the Heidelburg University, and the Lorbourne and was graduated at Gottingen in 1870, receiving the two degrees of Doctor of Philosophy, [and Master of Liberal Arts. In 1871 was professor of Latin and Greek in Lowell Seminary, Mass. In 1872 accepted a call to the

University of Minnesota, where the principal department was the German language and literature. In 1875 he was called to the chair of Intellectual Philosophy and Rhetoric in Lawrence University, which he still holds. Besides these branches he has had charge of the German classes, and has taught also in Greek, Latin, History, Evidences of Christianity, Moral Philosophy, Political Economy, Logic and Elocution. Is a member of the American Philological Society, the Wisconsin Academy of Arts and Sciences and the Philosophical Society of Great Britain. · He occasionally preaches, lectures, and writes for the press, but gives his time chiefly to the routine duties of his chair. Has a wife and two children. Prof. Sawyer is one of the ablest educators in the West."

SHREWSBURY SAWYERS.

I have striven in vain two full years to obtain facts about
the Shrewsbury Sawyers. At length I have received the following information from my valued friend and acquaintance of almost
fifty years ago, Capt. Joab Hapgood of Shrewsbury:

SHREWSBURY, JAN. 27, 1882.

There are now but two families of Sawyers in Shrewsbury.
Ward's history of Shrewsbury describes four families of that name,
which he thinks originated in Lancaster. The first was Aaron Sawyer,
who had three children born in Shrewsbury, Dolly, Elizabeth and
Aaron. This family is now extinct. The second was Oliver Sawyer,
who was published to Martha Hinds, Feb. 23, 1785, and there is no
other record of him in this town. The third was Calvin Sawyer, who
came from Sterling to Shrewsbury a widower with six children, but
was one of the Lancaster Sawyers. He next married Mary, daughter
of Samuel Burton, and had seven children born in Shrewsbury and in
Lancaster. Mr. Franklin A. Sawyer, who is a son of Calvin, now lives
in Shrewsbury, and is the only one of the family now in town. I
called on Mr. Franklin A. Sawyer, who was unable to give any further
information of his family than that in Ward's History. I enquired
what his grandfather's name was and he answered that he did not
know, by which I inferred that he chose not to communicate for special
reasons, and I asked no more questions. Calvin Sawyer's two oldest
sons, who came to Shrewsbury, settled in Providence and are now deceased. Caroline, the youngest child of Calvin, married Samuel
Houghton, who is now City Weigher at the Hay Market in Worcester. William Sawyer is the fourth mentioned in Ward's History. He
was a brother of Calvin, and lived but a short time after coming to
Shrewsbury. William had three daughters only, one of which is now
a widow, and living in Shrewsbury. I have called on her; she says
she thinks her family came from Lancaster, but when she was young.
Her grandfather's name was Joseph. I have called on Capt. Leander
Sawyer, who came to Shrewsbury after Ward's History was published.
His father's name was Alpheus, and his grandfather's name was also
Alpheus, and they came from Lancaster to Shrewsbury, so that all the
the Sawyers in Shrewsbury originated in Lancaster.

Yours Respectfully,   JOAB HAPGOOD.

All the above Sawyers were descendants from Joseph Sawyer
of Sawyer's Mills, who was the son of Thomas Sawyer, Jr., of
Lancaster, with the exception of Capt. Leander Sawyer, who was

15

a descendant of the youngest brother of Thomas Sawyer, Jr., whose name was Nathaniel. Alpheus Sawyer is in the record of the Sterling Sawyers by Dea. Samuel Sawyer of Sterling. Aaron Sawyer was the son of Aaron Sawyer, Sen., of Sawyer's Mills. His daughter Dolly married Col. Hezekiah Gibbs, and was the mother of Gen Aaron Sawyer Gibbs of Leominster; also of Dolly Sawyer Gibbs, who married Moses Woods. His son Aaron died when twenty years of age. There were three other brothers. One of them graduated from College and settled in Texas. The other two settled at Sawyer's Mills, one of them whose name was Joseph was the father of Caleb Sawyer of Clinton, Ezra Sawyer, of Worcester, and two other brothers who married Howe sisters in Holden. Oliver Sawyer, who was published to Martha Hinds, did marry her, and she was known as Patty Hinds ; those two names signifying the same person. They had a daughter Patty who married Joshua Kendall, and was the mother of O. Sawyer Kendall, now deceased. Calvin and William Sawyer were sons of Joseph Sawyer, Jr., of Sawyer's Mill's. They had three brothers named Joseph. Jabez and Thomas. Joseph graduated from Williamstown, and was settled as minister in Leverett, Mass., and died there in 1830, and was among the Alumni in Williams College. Jabez is now in New Salem, Mass , and a letter from him, giving his lineage, is in the preceding history. The reason that Aaron Sawyer, who was Aaron, Jr., and Oliver Sawyer, were contained in Ward's History of Shrewsbury, was because the Shrewsbury line at that time ran through Sawyer's Mills village, and the Sawyers on the south side of that line were in Shrewsbury, while those on the north side were in Lancaster, but they were all descendants of the same family, whose first parent was Joseph Sawyer, the son of Thomas, Jr., of Lancaster. He built the Sawyer's Mills between the years 1721 and 1753. When Boylston was incorporated as a town, it was composed of the northern portion of Shrewsbury and the southern portion of Lancaster, and thus the whole of Sawyer's Mills village was thereafter in the town of Boylston. This explains why the publishment of Oliver Sawyer and Martha Hinds was recorded in Shrewsbury, and probably the marriage was recorded in Boylston. The residence of Calvin and William Sawyer still remained in

Shrewsbury after Boylston was set off from it. Joseph Sawyer, the father of Calvin and William Sawyer, married Tabathy Prescott, the daughter of John Prescott, Jr., of Lancaster ; hence the Shrewsbury Sawyers were an extension of the Sawyer and Prescott families, who were among the first settlers in Lancaster. Joseph Sawyer, Sen., married Abigail Beaman, the daughter of John Beaman, and grand-daughter of Bezaleel Beaman, who was one of the first seven settlers, who settled in that part of the second purchase of Lancaster, which in 1781 was incorporated as the town of Sterling. Five of those seven settlers were sons of Nathaniel Sawyer, who was the youngest son of Thomas Sawyer, Sen., of Lancaster ; and one of them, Col. Ephraim Sawyer, commanded a regiment at the battle of Bunker Hill. The daughter of Joseph Sawyer, Sen., married Ephraim Houghton. He was a farmer near Sawyer's Mills. The bears and the deer troubled his corn-field, and he set a log-trap and caught the bear. He afterwards went out with his gun between sun down and dark to watch for deer around his corn-field. Seeing something move down beside his field, he fired upon it and killed his own son who happened to be there. Moses Sawyer, brother to Joseph Sawyer, Jr., and uncle to Calvin and William Sawyer, of Shrewsbury, settled in what is now Clinton. It was Lancaster during his life time. He married Lucy Larkin, sister of John Larkin, of Berlin, whose place of residence for many years was in the town of Lancaster. Old deeds, which were sent in for me to examine, proved the fact that Moses Sawyer, at different times, owned nearly all the land on which now stands the town of Clinton. He had a large family of children, five of them at least were sons, and four or five daughters. The widow of Moses Sawyer administered his estate, as was proved by one of the deeds sent in to me, which contained the name of Ephraim and Mary Sawyer, who conveyed inherited real estate in Sterling to the administratrix to enable her to make a conveyance of the whole. Miss Catherine Larkin of Berlin, who is cousin to the Moses Sawyer children, informs me that three of the sons died ; two of them being drowned by the up-setting of a boat. The third one righted the boat and crawled into it, but the oar being lost he had to paddle ashore with his hands, but became so chilled after he got ashore that he could not walk and had to crawl home. He was so enfeebled by the chill that he died soon afterwards. There was a son by the name of Peter, and he had a son Peter, who now lives in Clinton. There was a daughter who married a Rice, and was the mother of Abel Rice, now of Clinton. The widow lived to be ninety-five years of age. There were three minor daughters, and John Larkin was their guardian. One of them married Ephraim Hastings, and had a son and a daughter. The son, Capt. Christopher Sawyer Hastings, commanded a company in the Union Army during the late war ; and died of fever while in service. His body was brought home, and buried under arms with military honors. Another daughter married Stephen Wilder. I have seen them and two of their daughters, but was not personally acquainted with them. The third daughter married Ebenezer Wilder, and had five children, three sons and two daughters. With the three sons I was intimately acquainted. Their names were Ebenezer, Joseph and Sidney. The last time I recollect of seeing Joseph he was on duty as a line officer in the Lancaster Light Infantry. Sidney was a schoolmate of mine. Among the old deeds found in the old Moses Sawyer house, while being taken down a few years ago, was a Lieutenant's Commission given by the Lord High Admiralty of England, creating him a lieutenant in the British Army, to receive which he had to make oath to support the British Government ; hence very probably we do not find his name among the Revolutionary heroes. It is said the bears troubled his corn ; he set a steel trap and caught a young bear ; he went to the field with his gun, and, seeing the young bear in the trap, concluded the mother was not far off ; his gun being loaded he put a bullet in his mouth and poured a charge of powder in his hand, he shot the young bear and was able to re-load his gun and be in readiness for the old bear when she came to look after her cub.

An article in the *Clinton Courant* recently stated that Moses Sawyer and his brother Aaron were born in England ; that was a mistake ; they were born at Sawyer's Mills, which was then in Lancaster, and they were grand-sons of Thomas Sawyer, Jr., who was the first Sawyer ever born in Lancaster. Their mother was Abigail, daughter of John Beaman, then of Lancaster, and the Probate Records corroborate the fact.

MILITARY CHAPTER OF THE LANCASTER SAWYERS.

I had almost despaired of a military chapter; but I now have it from Mrs. Milton Baker of Brattleborough, Vt. It is compiled from the *Vermont Gazeteer*, and will be entered in full in the following pages. It seems there were three Col. Sawyers from Massachusetts in the Revolutionary Army. They all of them settled in Vermont after the war. They seemed to have dropped down among the Green Mountains, and were lost sight of in Massachusetts. Col. Ephraim Sawyer, of Lancaster, com- manded the Worcester County regiment at the battle of Bunker Hill, and also at battles of Saratoga. He had four sons who enlisted as officers in the Revolutionary Army, and one of them, Col. James L. Sawyer, commanded an infantry regiment at the battle of Yorktown. He was at the storming of the redoubt, fought by the side of Alexander Hamilton, formed an acquaint- ance with Gen. Lafayette, and was recognized by him at Burling- ton, in 1825. Col. Thomas Sawyer, of Bolton, who was the Mill- Wright, and built the first mill ever built in Bolton. When the war broke out he went immediately to the front, and was chief constructor of the breast works at Breed's Hill. He afterwards commanded a military company at Rutland, Vermont, and was stationed at Fort Ticonderoga after its capture by Ethan Allen. He and Col. James L. Sawyer both settled at Rutland, Vermont, after the war. Col. Ephraim Sawyer removed with his family and settled in Grand Isle County, Vermont, and died there. The Sawyers in Vermont were chiefly descendants from those three Revolutionary Colonels. They were very naturally a military race, as will be seen as by the record, compiled by Mrs. Baker. One of them graduated from Burlington, enlisted into the navy, and became Secretary to Commodore McDonough. He afterwards served on board the Frigate Cumberland twenty-one years, and was purser when he came out from service. Another Sawyer, a graduate from Burlington, married Miss Shaler of Middleton, Conn., and in seven weeks after was on his way to the Mediter-

ranean, in the ship Warren, to take part in the Tripolian war
A more particular account of the Vermont Sawyers will be found
in the communication from Mrs. Milton Baker, which here
follows:

LETTER FROM MRS. MILTON BAKER.

MR. CARTER:—In the "Vermont Historical Gazeteer," a magazine
embracing a history of each town, I find in volume 1st, page 36, in
the town of Goshen, Caledonian County, in 1815, Amos Sawyer and
Fanny Sawyer, his wife, were baptized with five others, and constitut-
ed the First Christian Church ; and on page 91, in the town of Salisbury there is the name of Col. Thomas Sawyer, a native of Bolton,
Mass., who engaged in milling till the Revolution, in which he at once
enlisted, and was master workman in constructing the fort at Bunker
or Breed's Hill. He afterwards commanded a company at Rutland,
Vt., and the Fort of Ticonderoga, after its capture by Allen. The
following December he led a company from thence to Rutland, through
a heavy fall of snow, in which some of the men, exhausted by the
march, sank down during the night and were frozen by the way. Seeing
his men fast losing heart, the following story is told of him : He bade
them hold on a little longer—there was a house just ahead where he had
ordered a warm supper. This roused them so that they pushed bravely on till they came to the house, when, finding the supper a hoax, they
were so warmed with anger that they were enabled to reach Rutland
without more loss by freezing.

He was afterwards stationed, with fifteen men, in a block house at
Shelburne, which was attacked in the night by a band of fifty-seven
Tories and Indians; but the history of this siege and brave defence we
will reserve for the history of Shelburne, to which it more properly belongs. In 1783, the Colonel came down Otter Creek to the mouth of a
tributary now called Leicester river, and followed up that stream in
quest of a mill privilege, till he come to the present site of Salisbury
village, which was then claimed to be in Leicester. Here he determin-
ed to build a grist-mill, and returning to Rutland he dressed his own
millstones from rocks in the vicinity, took them in two canoes, and
sending his son, (the father of E. Sawyer, now of Leicester,) with a
yoke of oxen through the woods, by the way of marked trees and a
compass, to meet him at their destination, he proceeded to his new loca-
tion, and erected a grist-mill and saw-mill. Some of the timbers now
remain where he put them. Before the boundary line between the

towns was established, he was regarded by Leicester as belonging to them, and he represented that town in the legislature three years. About the year 1800, he removed to Farmington, N. Y., where he died in about two years. The name of his wife wasEunice Carpenter. They had nine children. The Colonel was a man whose traits of character can be best learned by his acts.

On page 96, in the town of Shoreham, there is the name of Ephr. Sawyer, distinguished as a preacher (Baptist,) who was very successful in his labors from 1813 to 1816. Truly a zealous man and devoted servant of his Master; he is still held in grateful remembrance.

On page 497, the name of Col. James Sawyer appears. Born in 1762, he was the youngest son of Col. Ephraim Sawyer, of Lancaster, Mass.,who with his four sons served in the war of the Revolution,and were regular officers in the army. The father, Col. Eph. Sawyer, command- ed the Worcester County Regiment at the battle of Bunker Hill, and at the battles of Saratoga in 1777, after which he retired from service, but continued to support his sons there. James Sawyer, the son, was at the taking of Yorktown, and at the storming of the redoubt (put up to protect the wings.) He was an officer in the Massachusetts line. He was at the side of Col. Alex. Hamilton, to whose regiment of Light Infantry he belonged. After the Revolution he came to Rutland and lived four years. At the Rutland Shay's Rebellion he commanded the cavalry, and rendered important services in suppressing that outbreak. From Rutland he removed to Brandon, where he remained six years and removed to Burlington in 1796, where the first two years he was a merchant; and for six years thereafter, sheriff of the county. Mr. Sawyer married, in 1791, Lydia Foster of Clarendon. They and seven children. Mr. Sawyer died in Burlington in 1827. When Lafayette visited Burlington, he with others, who came to grasp the hand of their distinguished guest, passed up in silence, but the Roman nose and marked countenance, though it had been 42 years since they had met, were instantly recognized by the general, who saluted him without hes- itation, by his military title and name, remarking : "Time has made some changes with us all, sir."

. James L. Sawyer, son of James sawyer, graduated at Burlington, (Vermont University,) in 1806—then the youngest person who had ever graduated at this college. He was a lawyer by profession; he went to New York in 1829, where he spent the remainder of his days, and died in 1850. Frederick Augustus Sawyer, 1st Lieutenant of the 11th Vt. Regiment, in the war of 1812, son of James Sawyer, was as much of a soldier as any man I ever saw. He graduated from Vt.University just before the war, and entered the army as an ensign ; was in the battles of Chrystler's fields, Chippewa, Bridgewater, and in the defence of, and sortie from, Fort Erie. His regiment was six years after the war at Plattsburg, N. Y. In 1819 he resigned his commission, came out of the army with a high reputation, returned to Burlington, and here died in 1834.

Of Capt. Horace B. Sawyer, son of James Sawyer, honorable mention is made in the Chittenden Co., Military Chapter.

George F. Sawyer, son of James Sawyer, entered the Navy with Com. McDonough as Private Secretary. He was purser when he ied in 1852, on the Cumberland Frigate, recently destroyed by the Merrimac. He understood many languages and was in the Navy 28 years.

On page 66, I find the name of Isaac Sawyer, who with limited means for education, became a Baptist preacher. He was ordained in a barn, Sept. 24, 1798, and became a noted preacher of power and ability. He had several sons who became preachers of the Baptist order. He died a few years since in Jay, N. Y.

On page 581, I find in the Chittenden Co. Military Chapter, an account of Capt H. B. Sawyer that I have spoken of 'on this page. He says he entered the Navy June 4, 1812. Of that band of skillful and heroic officers, who in the French and Tripolitan wars, established the Navy in the confidence and affections of the American people, the number that remains is small and rapidly diminishing. To this class Capt. Horace Bucklin Sawyer belongs. He belonged to a military race. His grandfather, Col. Eph. Sawyer, having commanded Whitcomb's Worcester Co. Regiment at Bunker Hill and Saratoga, furnished four sons who were officers in the Revolution, spent an ample estate in the cause as the wont of the times was ; left Lancaster, Mass.. in 1786, with his numerous family, and emigrated to Grand Isle Co., Vt. His father, Col. James Sawyer, one of the four sons referred to, removed from Brandon to Burlington in 1786, where his third son was born Feb. 22, 1797. He was appointed by Hon. Martin Chittenden, then a member of Congress, as was also his brother, Frederick A. Sawyer. He married Miss Shaler from Middleton, Ct., and six weeks afterwards was on his way to the Mediterrean in the Warren. He was a man of strong mind and ready perception ; he was fond of books, and his information was extensive and accurate ; and his large acquaintance with society had given him manners courteous and winning ; singularly free from bad habits and vices, his tastes and pleasures were simple, manly and plain ; he liked to seek out the old soldiers and to do something for their benefit. In his domestic relations he was faultless, and he was loved by his family as few men have been, and he deserved it all. To that group he has left the memory of counsels, and the guidance of his example.

MRS. MILTON BAKER.